D0886760

Lobbying Together

Interest Group Coalitions in Legislative Politics

Kevin W. Hula

GEORGETOWN UNIVERSITY PRESS / WASHINGTON, D.C.

Georgetown University Press, Washington, D.C. 20007
© 1999 by Georgetown University Press. All rights reserved.

10 9 8 7 6 5 4 3 2 1   1999

THIS VOLUME IS PRINTED ON ACID-FREE ⊗ OFFSET BOOK PAPER

Library of Congress Cataloging-in-Publication Data

Hula, Kevin W.
    Lobbying together: interest group coalitions in legislative
politics / Kevin W. Hula.
        p.   cm. — (American governance and public policy)
    Includes bibliographical references and index.
    1. Lobbying—United States. 2. Pressure groups—United States.
3. Coalition (Social sciences) I. Title. II. Series.
JK1118.H85 1999
324′.4′0973—dc21
ISBN 0-87840-720-0 (cloth).
ISBN 0-87840-721-9 (pbk.)   98-44648

*For Sue and Megan
and for Harold, Anne, and Chris Hula*

Contents

Acknowledgments

As I think back over the years that have passed since I undertook this project, it is clear that I could never have completed it without the help of many, many people along the way.

I am deeply endebted to the 130 Washington representatives who offered me their time and their insight on coalition building.

I am grateful for Allan Cigler and Burdett Loomis at the University of Kansas, who not only pointed me toward the study of interest groups as an undergraduate, but have served as both friends and advisers for well over a decade.

I am grateful to Mo Fiorina, Jeff Berry, Jim Alt, and Mark Peterson for their excellent advice, patient counsel, and helpful commentary on my dissertation committee. I could never have gotten this project off the ground without Jeff's thoughtful encouragement and guidance during the development, research, and writing stages. Very helpful comments were provided by Katherine Tate, Paul Peterson, Pat Wolf, David Renelt, Thomas Stewart, Jessica Korn, Sam Mitchell, Byron Winn, John Owen, and Dan Philpott at various stages of the project at Harvard. Panel discussants Frank Baumgartner, William Browne, Doug Imig, and Karen McCurdy provided particularly helpful comments on earlier versions of some of these chapters at various conferences.

I am thankful for the financial support of the Jacob Javits Fellowship from the Department of Education at the earliest stages of this research. During the course of my research in Washington, the Brookings Institution generously placed a plethora of both tangible and intangible resources at my disposal by granting me special guest privileges in 1991–1992 and a Brookings Research Fellowship in 1992–1993. I am grateful for that assistance. Thank you also to my fellow research fellows, particularly John Bader, Ann Lin, and Wendy Schiller, for their support and helpful comments.

Loyola College in Maryland provided me with wonderful colleagues in Michael Franz, Janine Holc, Bill Kitchin, Hans Mair, Diana Schaub, and Don Wolfe in the Department of Political Science. Their encouragement, support, and help in developing this manuscript were invaluable. Mark Peyrot of the Loyola College Department of Sociology provided me with statistical advice at a critical stage in the project. Deans David Roswell and John Hollwitz provided crucial financial support during the last phases of the research. I am grateful to each of you.

Thank you to Brenda Marshall for her patience and assistance transcribing and typing many of the final interview transcripts.

Chapters 3 and 4 of this book grew out of a chapter published in the fourth edition of Cigler and Loomis's *Interest Group Politics*. The revised and expanded material is used here with the permission of Congressional Quarterly Press.

At Georgetown University Press I would like to thank John Samples, the anonymous readers who offered very helpful comments and criticism on the initial manuscript, and the helpful and capable staff in the production office.

I am grateful to all my family in Kansas, but especially my parents, Harold and Anne Hula, and my brother, Chris, for their support and encouragement. I am also profoundly thankful for my wife, Susan Hula, for her love, assistance, support, and immeasurable patience throughout this project. Megan Joyce Hula was a joyful distraction in the completion of this project, but the prospect of spending more time with her has been a tremendous incentive to finish it. I love you all.

Most important, I can only express a truly humble thankfulness to the Lord for His guidance, grace, and mercy.

Thank you to these, and to all others who assisted me at different stages in this project. All errors in the manuscript were, of course, mine in the first place and remain mine today.

Lobbying Together

1

A New Look at Coalition Building

INTRODUCTION

Religious persecution is not an activity that has a lot of supporters on Capitol Hill, and when a bill was introduced in 1997 to place sanctions on countries that persecuted religious minorities, it seemed like a winner to many observers outside the Washington Beltway. However, the old adage that politics makes strange bedfellows is nowhere more true than among the organized interests represented in Washington. A coalition of twelve trade associations, including the Newspaper Association of America, the Nonprescription Drug Manufacturers Association, the National Food Processors Association, and the National Soft Drink Association, formed to voice serious concerns about the bill.[1] Since none of these organizations advocated religious persecution, what was it that pulled them together to lobby as a coalition? Gum arabic.

Gum arabic is a naturally occurring substance derived from the acacia tree that is used in many food products, cosmetics, newspaper printing, and other everyday items. The problem that mobilized the coalition is that between 70 and 90 percent of the world's supply of gum arabic comes from Sudan, a major target of the bill. A strong bill cutting off trade with Sudan would have a tremendous impact on the users of gum arabic, for which there is no artificial substitute. When a small importer noticed an article discussing the problem of religious persecution in Sudan and the proposed sanctions bill, he began calling trade association representatives to alert them to the danger.

President Clinton preempted legislative action in November 1997 by issuing an executive order banning trade with Sudan. While freezing Sudan's assets in the United States and banning American investment in Sudan, the order expressly noted that licenses might be issued for the importation of products like gum arabic, for which there were no other sources.

The broader connection between economic sanctions and religious persecution has captured the attention of USA*Engage, a coalition of over 600 businesses unified by their opposition to unilaterally imposed sanctions. Each of these organizations has an economic interest that is challenged to some degree by proposed bills that would limit trade with countries where they do business. For some, like PepsiCo, the economic interest might be the need for gum arabic from Sudan. For others, like Boeing, it might be the sale of aircraft in China. Even a bill that appeared non-controversial at first blush can attract the attention (and opposition) of dozens or even hundreds of Washington representatives within a very short time.

ORGANIZED INTERESTS AND
WASHINGTON REPRESENTATIVES

Washington is a city of representatives. Though some of them are elected to represent a geographic constituency in Congress, most Washington representatives represent corporations, membership groups, industries, and institutions. Still others represent demographic slices of the American pie or simply an ideological position. Almost all of them share one thing, though: regardless of their budget, visibility, reputation, or past experiences, few of them consistently work alone. Organized interests fight their major battles today largely in coalitions. Lobbying coalitions are also the building blocks out of which political consensus within the Washington Beltway is built.

News headlines from the legislative trenches recount the conflict and cooperation surrounding coalitions. Conflict caught the journalist's attention when the U.S. Chamber of Commerce, the National Association of Manufacturers, and the National Association of Wholesaler-Distributors, among others, allied themselves in a multifront assault on tobacco legislation, fearing that it would strengthen the trial lawyers if passed.[2] Cooperation was the apparent emphasis when organizations representing airlines, aircraft manufacturers, and pilots formed a coalition to change the agenda for future safety legislation.[3] Although such news reports are commonplace in national newspapers, we know relatively little about interest group coalitions, when they are most likely to form, and which activities organized interests are most likely to pursue alone or in concert. To understand interest group interaction we need to explore these coalitions, examining not only the relationships that develop among organizations but the specific incentives that pull organizations together or lead them to work independently in the policy arena.

This is a book about why coalition strategies have emerged as a dominant lobbying technique among Washington representatives and how these strategies affect the activities that individual Washington representatives pursue as they participate in the national policy process.

Fragmentation in a Changing Environment

The Washington representative's job is multifaceted. In addition to keeping tabs on legislation and regulations related to their organization, representatives need to convey the needs, desires, and interests of their organization to the government, to other organizations, to the media, and to the public. For a number of reasons explored in this book, these responsibilities have become increasingly difficult to carry out successfully as the policy process and the political environment have changed. Washington representatives have responded by turning to coalition strategies—entering into symbiotic alliances with other organizations to facilitate their own goals in the policy process.[4]

The changes in the interest group universe over the last four decades have been astonishing. The level of interest group activity in Washington has exploded. The number of national associations has grown from approximately five thousand in 1955 to over twenty-three thousand at the end of the twentieth century.[5] New public interest groups have formed to represent consumers, environmental concerns, and welfare interests, among others.[6] The number of interest groups with a foreign policy agenda has expanded rapidly, and the number of business and trade associations, already high as a proportion of organized interests, has skyrocketed as well.[7] Today there are well over three times more corporations with a full-time Washington office than there were just thirty years ago.[8] Scholars have viewed the proliferation of interests as indicative of a fragmented and atomistic political system.[9] This macroview of the interest group community, however, often overlooks a number of institutional links between interest groups, most notably the increasing use of long-term, recurrent, and institutionalized coalitions in many policy arenas. Kay Schlozman and John Tierney report that

> coalitions among private organizations seem to be not simply an important, but an increasingly important, component of Washington politics. Sixty-seven percent of our respondents indicated that their organizations had increased their commitment to coalitional activity over the past decade. In terms of increasing use by Washington organizations, entering into coalitions ranks second on the list of 27 techniques of influence.[10]

Although interest group scholars have documented the presence and activities of lobbying coalitions through policy case studies, no comprehensive study has been published to investigate the broader scope of interest group coalitions and explain their roles as institutions of collective leadership, bargaining, and strategy for member organizations. This is perhaps not surprising, given that political scientists generally understand the atomized political environment in terms of Hugh Heclo's model of issue networks. Heclo successfully challenged the traditional model of subgovernments and iron triangles, arguing that it was "not so much wrong as it was disastrously incomplete."[11] Iron triangle models claimed that many policy areas were dominated by small sets of political actors working in impermeable, long-term relationships. The triangles included a peak interest group, a Congressional committee, and the relevant executive branch agency. In its most extreme form, the iron triangle model suggested that policy might emerge from a deal cut by a lobbyist, a committee chair, and a regulatory official. Heclo pointed out that policies emerged from an environment where political relationships were more numerous, permeable, and transient than the iron triangle model allowed. In dismissing theories of subgovernments, Heclo forced political scientists to take a harder look at the complexities of interest group politics. Thomas Gais, Mark Peterson, and Jack Walker have documented the breakdown of the traditional subgovernment model, and several excellent studies have been conducted to develop the issue network concept.[12] However, the issue network concept was not intended to answer all of our questions about interest group interaction.

At an empirical level, Heclo's description of issue networks is a "theory of non-structure" for interest group interaction, featuring an atomistic view of interest groups as a set of independent actors who interact unpredictably on the basis of shared expertise and knowledge about issues. By atomistic, I do not mean that Heclo portrayed groups as political actors who did not interact or cooperate. By definition, a network is created by interaction. However, the interaction between groups under the network model is (and under Heclo's premise *must be* because of its very nature) uncharted, imprecise, and undefined.

Unlike the iron triangle model, which posited close, finite, and long-term relationships, an issue network is composed of groups that come and go as issues and specific policy debates change and develop. Discussing the membership of an issue network with certainty is oxymoronic, because well-versed individuals and groups float through networks as issues rise and fall. Heclo writes, "What does an issue network look like? It is difficult to say precisely, for at any given time only one part of a network may be active and through time the various connections may intensify or fade among the policy intermediaries and the executive and congressional bureaucracies."[13] Furthermore, Heclo argues specifically not only that there are many groups and individuals active in a network, but that there are many issue networks active on interrelated issues. "For example, there is no single health policy network but various sets of people knowledgeable and concerned about cost-control mechanisms, insurance techniques, nutritional programs, prepaid plans, and so on."[14] In essence, the very definition of the issue network makes it devoid of boundaries and predictive power. As Heclo himself states: "Issue networks . . . comprise a large number of participants with quite variable degrees of mutual commitment or of dependence on others in their environment; in fact it is almost impossible to say where a network leaves off and its environment begins. . . . Participants move in and out of the networks constantly."[15]

Robert Salisbury goes so far as to label the political environment today "a destabilized world of fragmented interests and multidimensional challenges from externality groups."[16] It is this movement of individuals and groups in and out of both issues and networks that I refer to in this book with the term "atomization."

In their magisterial work on Washington representatives, interests, and policy domains, John Heinz and his colleagues underscored the fragmented state of issue networks through the metaphor of a political community with a "hollow core." Through in-depth interviews with political notables, the research team sought to identify dominant policy actors who were active in meaningful ways across many issue domains. Not only were there no core actors *across* issue networks, but the authors reported a lack of core actors *in any* of the four issue domains they examined: "[I]n all of the domains we find little evidence to suggest that a powerful role is played by intermediaries—by more or less autonomous actors who are able to use their personal influence to promote compromise or impose settlements."[17]

Group proliferation, atomization, and policy domains with hollow cores have a common effect. Without core actors to coordinate political action within a policy domain, the use of coalitions has become more important to lobbyists.

Coalitions

Though all coalitions are characterized by organizational actors cooperatively pursuing political goals, coalitions are crafted in many different forms. Some coalitions, such as the Committee for Education Funding, have been around for many years. These formal, long-term coalitions are almost indistinguishable from an interest group with organizational members. Other coalitions are much less formal and may only exist for a short time to protest or support a specific piece of legislation. In some cases, these short-term coalitions may not even take on a name. In the summer of 1997, for example, the Congress considered a tax hike on airline passengers. Given two competing plans before the conference committee, seven major airlines chose to support a plan that would shift a portion of their current air travel tax burden to smaller, low-fare carriers. The seven carriers (American, Continental, Delta, Northwest, Trans World, United, and US Airways) staged a rally on the west front of the Capitol with over one thousand of their employees in attendance.[18] This informal coalition was intended to demonstrate unity to the conference committee.

As it currently stands, the issue network view of interest group interaction is simply too amorphous to explain and differentiate between the regular, institutionalized cooperation of formal interest group coalitions, like the Committee for Education Funding, and the short-term, rapidly changing composition of informal coalitions like the seven airlines mentioned above. Yet it is through these coalitions that organized interests within an issue network often interact and mutual policy preferences are articulated.

Returning to the proverbial drawing board, tentative steps toward understanding the interaction between interest groups at the coalition level have been taken by a handful of scholars. Schlozman and Tierney, as well as Salisbury and his colleagues, note that groups tend to identify most of their "allies" as other groups within their issue or economic sector; for example, farm commodity groups find a plurality of their allies among other farm commodity groups.[19] These studies demonstrate that there are many stable, long-term relationships between allies and adversaries in the interest group universe. Burdett Loomis makes an important, if nonempirical, argument that the proliferation of interest groups in the last thirty years has actually stimulated more interest group collaboration.[20] Loomis also creates an analytic framework for interest group coalitions by differentiating them by longevity and breadth of concern, and by describing briefly how coalitions differ at different stages of the policy process. Virginia Gray and David Lowery borrow from behavioral ecology to describe coalition behavior in terms of animal-like foraging as an alternative to rational choice approaches prevalent in the collective action literature.[21] These works notwithstanding, the examination of coalition building among interest groups remains at a relatively primitive stage in comparison with other areas of interest group research, such as campaign expenditures by political action committees (PACs).

The next step in understanding coalition behavior is the development of a model that can predict which groups will work together, why they coalesce, what their alliances will look like, and when these alliances will arise. We need to assess the differential impact of policy fields upon interorganizational relationships, cooperation, and collective action. Understanding the manner in which organizations cooperate and coordinate policy advocacy in political coalitions is a vital step in understanding the internal dynamics of an issue network.

Beyond expanding our understanding of issue networks, however, the study of coalitions can help us understand the nature of political conflict and compromise. Coalitions are arguably the central method for aggregating the viewpoints of organized interests in American politics. They serve as institutional mediators reconciling potentially disparate policy positions, in effect "predigesting" policy proposals before they are served to the legislature.[22]

GENERAL OVERVIEW OF THE PROJECT

There are two central purposes of this study. First, it will document, measure, and explain the conditions under which coalitions of organized interests arise, both within and between policy sectors, as well as across stages of the policy process. Second, I will argue that institutional links provide substantial advantages for organizations that desire to coordinate their political action with other organizations, and those without established *institutional* links to other organizations find it necessary to create new *behavioral* links—coalitions.

In chapter 2 I lay out the research methodology I have followed in this project. I discuss the choice of a long interview format, the sampling technique, the survey instrument, and the outline of the 130 interviews I conducted with interest group leaders and government affairs specialists.

Beginning in chapter 3 I examine group behavior and try to explain the decision calculus that group leaders make when deciding whether to act independently or in cooperation with other groups. Interest group leaders must decide whether to engage in political action independently, in unique temporary coalitions, in recurring temporary coalitions, or under the umbrella of permanent, institutionalized interest group coalitions. I show that there is an internally coherent rationale for the decisions group leaders make, in which outcomes can be explained by models of resource exchanges among purposive actors.

I argue that the nature and problems of collective action for group coalitions are somewhat different from the collective action problems for interest groups composed of individuals. In fact, the classic free-rider problem described by Mancur Olson may not be applicable to coalition building among established interest groups in most cases.[23] Groups join coalitions to pursue strategic goals at reduced costs, to shape public debate by influencing a coalition's platform, to gather information, and to receive symbolic benefits.

I continue to use the exchange model adopted in chapter 3 to examine coalition structure and organization in chapter 4. I argue that the distribution of internal and external incentives organizations seek in joining a coalition will determine both the ultimate structure of that coalition and the role that each group plays in that coalition, roles I conceptualize as "core members," "players," and "tag-alongs."

In chapter 5 I focus on institutional aspects of political coordination in the interest group universe. Before political action can be coordinated, a critical stage of intelligence collection must occur. Many groups are institutionally linked to one another through "one-way doors" and "group interlocks." These institutional links can provide effective conduits for the coordination of information exchange and group strategy. Organizations that are institutionally linked to one another have strategic advantages in intelligence gathering unavailable to groups without such links. Analysis of these links provides a theoretical basis with which to explain the role of what Loomis calls "coalition brokers."[24] Though these institutional links are not utilized on every issue, their very real presence creates a loose but generally stable framework of relationships within policy sectors that issue network models do not yet adequately take into account. Thus, I am able to explore the degree to which interest groups in three policy fields are or are not atomistic and independent as posited by Heclo's issue network model.

Chapter 6 presents a brief case study on a coalition with which several interview respondents were involved. This case study of the Coalition for the GSP (Generalized System of Preferences) not only highlights the usefulness of coalition strategies but also provides an important indication of the changes technology brings to the formation and maintenance of coalitions. Enhanced communications technology and expanded information availability have wide-reaching implications for coalition brokers and peripheral members alike.

I turn in chapter 7 to specific activities organizations perform in the political and policy arenas, and discuss *when* groups are most likely to pursue coalition strategies and when they are most likely to work alone. I use incentive theory to show how opportunities to develop reputation and political capital are the most important concerns in predicting when group leaders will participate in coalition behaviors. I do this by differentiating between the "enabling strategies" and "terminal goals" that groups pursue. Groups pursue strategies early in the game that will enable them to reach their terminal goals. The key enabling strategy revolves around developing a specific reputation through credit claiming and self-differentiation. Groups are able to differentiate themselves from other organizations most easily and with the lowest risk in the political arena rather than during policy debates. Coalitions, therefore, are much more likely to arise in the policy arena than in the political arena.

In chapter 8, I explore two questions regarding environmental opportunities for coalition building and the constraints that hold some groups back from coalition strategies. The first question is whether groups that are active in a number of different policy domains are more likely to be active coalition members than groups that participate in only one domain. My data suggest that this is the case. Second, I ask whether organizations' ideological and party preferences affect their participation in political coalitions. Group leaders that identify their organization as "liberal" report higher efficacy scores for collective action and coalition building than group leaders who label their organizations "conservative." However, conservatives are significantly more likely than liberals to report ease in forming long-term coalitions.

In the concluding chapter I review the research and conclusions of the book in light of James Madison's argument that a large republic will dilute the effects of societal factions.

2

Methods for the Study of Coalitions

STUDY DESIGN AND RESEARCH BOUNDARIES

The study of interest groups has traditionally utilized a blend of several streams of political science inquiry. Groups have been examined as institutions, as vehicles for political participation, and as forms of behavior.[1] Research methodologies vary widely as well. William Browne notes that most of the academic literature on interest groups falls into three general categories: broad theoretical treatments, case studies of single organizations, and "empirical behavioral studies of some universe of individuals involved with interest organizations."[2] Each of these approaches has significant methodological problems, though they bring important benefits into the intellectual discussion, to be sure.

As Browne notes, the broad theoretical treatments which best place the interest group universe into the larger political picture have frequently relied on anecdotal evidence from a hodgepodge of sources. Case studies of single organizations provide rich detail and powerful explanations for microlevel behavior, but it is difficult for a reader to satisfy the gnawing question of whether a particular case might represent the exception rather than the rule. The collection of macrolevel data across groups allows generalization, but Browne argues that it has often led to superficial conclusions about what lobbying actually accomplishes in specific contexts.[3]

Following the work of Henry J. Pratt, Browne suggests that the best way to minimize the problems associated with each methodology is to combine methodological approaches.[4] Pratt and Browne each study a broad range of organizations within a single policy sector. Pratt examines aging policy and Browne studies agriculture. This move shifts the level of analysis from a single organization to a policy domain, allowing groups within that domain to be compared with one another. A clearer picture of the policy process emerges. In studying group coalitions, Loree Bykerk and Ardith Maney use the single-policy-domain method to examine consumer groups on Capitol Hill.[5]

However, at the most basic level, studying one policy domain does not escape the central critique of the group-level case study; one must compare studies of more than one domain in order to recognize what is unique in each and what is general. To enable this type of comparison, I have adopted a multiple-domain approach for this study.[6] Rather than selecting one policy domain for an in-depth study, I pursued in-depth interviews with dozens of organizational representatives in three policy domains: transportation, education, and civil rights. This strategy enabled me to "soak and poke," exploring coalition building through the eyes of participants while keeping a watchful eye out for behavioral differences that may arise between different domains.

The data examined here represent 130 in-depth interviews conducted with Washington representatives from corporations, associations, unions, and other organizations that had actively lobbied the 101st Congress in any of the three policy spheres.

This study of coalition formation is exploratory in nature. Given the dearth of basic research on coalition formation among organized interests in Washington, it was necessary not only to develop new hypotheses but also to collect and analyze an entirely new dataset that focused specifically on coalition formation and participation.

In the rest of this chapter I will lay out my rationale for conducting fieldwork and face-to-face interviews, give a brief overview of the policy domains, and discuss the research design, including the sampling procedures, survey instrument, and interviewing procedures.

Rationale for Fieldwork

Interest group research generally involves extended fieldwork in Washington.[7] There are several reasons for this, the most significant being the traditional lack of access to large interest group datasets comparable to the datasets dealing with the census, elections, or roll call votes.[8] In recent years, some data have been made available to the research community through ICPSR, most notably the 1980/1985 panel data from Jack Walker's survey of organized interest groups and the Heinz et al. survey of Washington representatives and employers conducted in 1982–83.[9] However, in general there is a dearth of qualitative and quantitative data about coalition activities and the opinions of interest group leaders regarding various forms of coalition strategies. The data available when I undertook this project did not have the extensive information on coalitions and coalition building I required.

The lack of readily available data pertaining to the formation of political coalitions among interest groups is not surprising in many respects. Aside from the general dearth of quantitative interest group data, journalistic accounts of coalition activities are uneven and are not comparable in the absence of control variables.

Primary documents and first-party accounts of coalition strategy and behavior were clearly preferable to secondary accounts, which were either unavailable, irrelevant, or insufficient for this study. However, there is no easy way to compile primary data about coalitions that are sufficiently in-depth and statistically comparable short of fieldwork. Groups themselves rarely publish objective accounts of their coalition behaviors, strategies, or other internal decisions. Whereas governmental institutions publish relatively clear rules and guidelines about the general outline of their decision-making processes,[10] the decision rules of organized interests are rarely publicized. As Allan Cigler notes: "Research is often made difficult because interest groups and associations are semiprivate or private entities sensitive about their visibility."[11] Decision making in an interest group generally takes place at the staff or board level. The decision-making process is generally closed to the public, and decisions of a strategic or tactical nature are seldom announced. There is no widely available interest group equivalent to the *Congressional Record*, the *Federal Register*, or the *United States Supreme Court Reporter*, which report decisions of governmental institutions. Group publications are available, though there is no guarantee that they will cover the topics that the researcher wishes to pursue in more than a cursory fashion, if at all.

Because this book focuses on the questions of decision making, incentives, and group strategies in coalitions, and because the variables I was interested in were not available elsewhere, it was necessary to collect original data in Washington myself. Personal interviews with interest group leaders about their involvement in coalitions seemed the most appropriate research strategy to pursue.

Plowing new intellectual ground can turn up both confirmations and surprises, and in this explicitly exploratory project, I have made every effort to remain open to both.

Domain Selection

The original research design called for two sets of interviews, the first set conducted with organizations that lobbied on transportation issues and the second set with organizations lobbying on education issues. After interviews with Washington representatives active in the transportation domain were begun, additional resources were made available that enabled me to expand the original research design to include a third sample of organizations lobbying on civil rights issues. Limiting the study to two or three issue areas was intended to enable a more detailed examination of the patterns of cooperation than a broader survey, potentially sampling all organized interests, would have. On the other hand, by examining more than one policy domain I was able to make direct comparisons between the domains based on the same variables.

A word of caution is in order: The reader who is looking for a detailed commentary on the substantive issues within these three policy areas will be disappointed. Ultimately this is not a book about education, transportation, and civil rights. It is a book about coalitions, why they form, and how interest group leaders use them. Examining the formation of coalitions in three domains, each of which displays different kinds of economic, ideological, and policy considerations, permits a comparison of institutional links and coalition mechanisms and an examination of the potential comparative advantages that economic competitors have over ideologically or policy-driven organizations when they engage in collective action.

The transportation, education, and civil rights issue domains were selected because they display significant differences in the composition of organized interests active in each domain and significant differences in the nature of the political issues addressed in each domain.

Transportation

The earliest political debates over transportation policy were constitutional in nature: did the government have the constitutional authority to undertake internal improvements such as the National Road? This debate continued in one form or another throughout the first third of the nineteenth century.[12] Private railways (many initially chartered by states) sprang up in the 1800s and dominated east-west transportation, leading to the creation of the Interstate Commerce Commission in 1887 and the passage of the Sherman Antitrust Act in 1890, as well as to significant debates over monopoly power in the late nineteenth and early twentieth centuries.[13] Since the Second World War transportation policy has been characterized by both distributional and regulatory politics.[14] Most of the key pieces of transportation-related legislation today concern construction projects or are part of the ongoing debate over the regulation and deregulation of transportation industries.[15] However, cutthroat economic and political competition continues between transportation sectors (e.g., between trucking and rail), as well as within transportation sectors (e.g., the airline industry).[16]

The issues addressed in the transportation domain are almost monolithically economic in nature. To amend Clausewitz freely, in this domain politics appears to be the extension of economics by other means. Two of the key regulatory issues of the 1970s and 1980s were the deregulation of the airline and trucking industries.[17] The 1990s brought about the creation of two of the most pork-filled surface transportation acts in history.

The transportation domain is characterized by heavy lobbying by business interests, primarily trade associations (such as the American Bus Association or the Air Transport Association) and corporations (such as UPS or American Airlines). Other key players, though less numerous than business interests, include state and local governments and government-related organizations like the National Association of Counties and the American Association of State Highway and Transportation Officials. Labor unions and ideological groups are active on transportation issues from time to time (for example, the Railway Labor Executives Association), though their attention is generally not on transportation policy per se.

Education

Prior to the Civil War, the federal government's support for education was primarily in the form of grants to the states of land and surplus tax money. Beginning with the Morrill Act of 1862 the federal government began identifying and financially supporting specific fields of study and forms of education.[18] This law was "the first enactment of national policy to grant federal support for specifically prescribed educational purposes."[19] By the end of the nineteenth century, publicly funded "common schools" had been established in every state in the Union.[20]

Most of the education policies in the United States are decided at the state and local level, but the federal government plays a critical budgetary role in several areas. Federal aid to education is important not only for supporting a common education for the public but also for collateral education programs. The federal government subsidizes both special educational programs for those with physical and learning disabilities and top-level research programs that have pushed back the frontiers of scientific and technical knowledge.

Numerous organizations lobby on behalf of Department of Education programs, particularly for student financial aid programs, special education programs, and university-based research and development funding. At the same time, there is a cadre of organizations active in Washington that lobby for the dismantling of the Department of Education, and still others take part in the perennial debates over national educational standards and school choice.

The education domain has also served as a battlefield for other debates, most notably the ongoing discussion of the sacred and the secular on issues such as school prayer and evolution. It has also been ground zero for critical chapters of the civil rights debates such as school and university desegregation, school busing, affirmative action admissions, and multicultural curricula.

Lobbying in the education domain is conducted primarily by three types of organizations: (1) professional organizations and unions, such as those representing principals, teachers, superintendents, college presidents, and financial aid administrators; (2) institutions, such as two- and four-year colleges, universities, and "Big Six" organizations that represent higher education;[21] and (3) governmental and quasi-governmental bodies, such as school boards, states, state departments of education, and the specialized organizations that represent those bodies.

Unlike the transportation domain, where debates are dominated by business interests, education policy is an area in which the business community plays a relatively small role. From time to time individual businesses or business coalitions take part in the educational policy debates, but this is rare and generally limited in duration. In some cases, for example, businesses may support higher educational standards to raise the competence of the pool of entry-level job applicants. Others, like the Edison Project, are attempting to develop privatized, for-profit ventures in public education.[22]

Civil Rights

The tenuous relationship between the races in America has been called the great "American dilemma," and few areas of public policy have been more contentious or more central to the evolving definition of who we are as a nation than the ongoing discussion over civil rights.[23] When most Americans hear the term "civil rights," they think of the relationship between white and black Americans. Indeed, the lasting legacy of two centuries of slavery in the United States can be seen in the differential educational levels, employment patterns, housing conditions, and political participation of white and black Americans today. Jim Crow laws and state-sponsored segregation, coupled with the widespread de facto denial of basic political rights for African-Americans after Reconstruction, are central elements in the context of civil rights discussions in the early and mid-twentieth century.[24]

However, the modern debate over civil rights also grows out of many other less frequently discussed chapters from American history, including the geographic displacement of Native Americans,[25] anti-Irish discrimination in the nineteenth century,[26] anti-German sentiment during the First World War,[27] and the forcible internment of many Japanese-Americans during the Second World War,[28] to name just a few. More recently addressed issues in the civil rights domain include the broad debates over gay rights[29] and defining civil rights for the disabled.[30]

Broad ideological issues as well as narrow economic issues are at stake in contemporary debates over civil rights policy. The key issues in this domain have traditionally included the enforcement of general political rights such as voting, nondiscrimination and desegregation in education, fair housing, and nondiscrimination in employment.[31] These broad issues can be conceptualized in a number of different types of public policy: regulatory (which would include, for example, bilingual education and the protection from discrimination in the workplace, housing, voting, and public facilities), distributive (including contract set asides and preferences), and redistributive (policies pursued through various welfare programs).

Political activity in the civil rights domain is generally characterized by a strong presence of organizations mobilized specifically to pursue and protect civil rights for specific demographic categories (such as the NAACP, the Japanese-American Citizens League, or the National Association for Women and Girls in Education), supported or opposed by a large number of externality groups that have a significant stake in a given piece of legislation or policy debate. Corporate America generally takes a keen interest in the economic effects civil rights legislation might have on the business sector and is vocal when it perceives costly regulation or quotas. Although the transportation and education domains have both had their share of strikes and protests, the civil rights domain clearly is more linked in the public eye to protest tactics and insurgency than the other two domains.[32]

Group Selection

Rather than attempting to capture all interorganizational relationships within the policy domains, I limited the study to relationships that exist among organizations active in the context of congressional lobbying in these three policy fields. Hence, I selected the sample for each policy field from a limited universe composed of all organizations offering testimony before any House or Senate committee or subcommittee hearing on any transportation, education, or civil rights issue over a two-year indexing cycle (testimonies during the 101st Congress). This included businesses, unions, public interest groups, professional associations, trade associations—any type of organized interest. Drawing the sample from testimony set an arbitrary minimum standard of group access for potential inclusion in the sample. The minimum standard is not particularly high, since at least one study demonstrated that 99 percent of the organizations active in Washington report testifying before Congress.[33] The effect of this restriction was more significant in creating a temporal parameter, identifying subpopulations active during a given two-year period. The total dataset is comprised of three samples, one for each policy area.

Each of these samples had two components, a randomly drawn sample and an additional subsample of the most frequently testifying organizations. This technique (horizontal and vertical nonproportional stratification) yielded more information for inter- and intrasector comparisons than a purely random sample would have,[34] enabling me to discuss the most active groups in some detail (the "core" groups in chapter 4) without losing the ability to generalize about the issue sectors. The resulting total sample represents organizations that are active in each policy sphere, but which need not be primarily identified with that sphere. For example, in the sample of organizations lobbying in the transportation domain, there are not only groups and firms representing "planes, trains, and automobiles" but also energy producers and safety advocates. Similarly, the education sample included trade unions interested in job training and computer manufacturers promoting the development of a technologically literate workforce.

DATA COLLECTION

Group Inclusion and Sampling Procedures

The specific selection procedures for organizations interested in education, transportation, and civil rights were almost identical. As noted above, I used appearance at a subcommittee or committee hearing as the minimum access threshold for inclusion on the list from which I drew my interviewing samples. I went through the Congressional Information Service (CIS) Index, and listed every hearing indexed under transportation-, education-, or civil rights-related topics. Transportation hearings were selected from all index entries related to moving people or goods by any means short of space travel.[35] A full listing of issue index entries is included in the endnotes. For the purpose of my search, I defined educational policy to include "Headstart" through "undergraduate" levels. Vocational, technical, and other parallel paths were also included, as were more abstract topics such as literacy.[36] I defined civil rights policy broadly, including not only race and ethnicity but also gender, as well as the rights of individuals with physical and mental disabilities. I did not, however, include general First Amendment civil liberties issues.[37]

After reading the abstract for each hearing, I included all organizations represented by witnesses, with specific exceptions as noted below:

1. no governments or government agencies (but I did include associations representing groups of governments or government workers);
2. no local groups (below the state level); for example, whereas

the Twin Falls, South Dakota, Chamber of Commerce would not have been included, the state-level South Dakota Chamber of Commerce would have been included;
3. no individual employees who are likely appearing as "examples" of their profession rather than as representatives of their employer or an association;
4. no schools, colleges, universities, or individual professors (unless they are representing a group or association).

I omitted the categories in item 4 from the education list, primarily to keep the same sampling rules as I used for transportation. The first three exclusionary rules listed above apply to most cases in which a university official testified before Congress. In fact, almost no individuals testified solely on behalf of a university. Most frequently, testimony by faculty members was offered because of their personal substantive expertise—for example, "John Doe, economist at M.I.T.," explaining the prospects for inflation. University administrators, much more likely candidates to represent the interests of their university, were listed generally as "John Doe, president of XYZ State University, representing National Association of State Universities and Land Grant Colleges." In all of these cases, the organization was added to the list.

There were 719 groups on the transportation list, 438 groups on the education list, and 282 groups on the civil rights list, from which the samples were drawn.[38] Numbers were assigned to each organization, and the random component of each sample was subsequently drawn using a table of random numbers.[39] The transportation and education random samples included fifty-five organizations. The ten most frequently testifying groups were added to this sample, yielding a list of sixty-five organizations that were contacted in these fields. Forty-five organizations were contacted in the civil rights sample, including the ten most frequently testifying groups.

THE INTERVIEWS

Procedures

Contacts and interviews were conducted on a rolling basis. The first wave of the transportation sample was contacted initially via letter explaining the research project and requesting an interview. Follow-up calls to set up the interview took place a week later. This method was dispensed with subsequently in favor of a pure telephone contact strategy for logistical reasons. Organizations not responding to the initial telephone call were called a second time approximately three weeks later. Groups not responding to that call were contacted a third time one month after the second call.

Given the changing time demands of organizational representatives and the ebb and flow of deadlines, the long lag time between the initial call and follow-up calls was meant to allow those who did not respond because they were facing deadlines to get past specific events confronting them.

Specific respondents were targeted at most groups in the sample on the basis of their job titles as listed in the most recent edition of *Washington Representatives* or other leads available at the time of contact.[40] I attempted to speak with the highest-level individual in governmental affairs who was personally active in lobbying and coalition activities. My first contacts were usually aimed at individuals who served as "director of government affairs," though the actual job titles of respondents ranged from legislative representative to executive director. Titles can be deceiving. It was not uncommon, given the "title inflation" of the Washington Beltway, to speak with the "vice president for governmental affairs" in an organization with a governmental affairs staff of two.

Transportation-related interviews were conducted from December 1991 through July of 1992. Education-related interviews were conducted from November 1992 through May of 1993. Civil rights-related interviews were conducted from February to August of 1993. Forty-nine interviews were conducted in the transportation sample, followed by fifty in the education sample and thirty-one interviews in the civil rights sample. The response rates were 75 percent in transportation, 77 percent in education, and 69 percent in civil rights.

In almost all cases, interviews were conducted face-to-face with a single respondent. There are several reasons I chose to use personal interview survey procedures. Personal interviews can provide both quantifiable data from closed-ended questions (enabling me to employ quantitative analysis) and broader answers to open-ended questions to help me refine and enrich the models I develop. While face-to-face interviews are more time-consuming than mailed survey instruments, the added depth and ability to probe seem particularly useful in an exploratory study attempting to understand and explain coalition behavior within issue networks. Indeed, face-to-face interviews are necessary to "tease out" the full extent of coalition relationships.[41] In one case a respondent told me after the interview that arranging an appointment was much more effective than mailing written questionnaires, which he said he regularly received and invariably threw away. I suspect that he was not the only interest group representative with that practice. In three cases, interviews were actually conducted over the phone at the request of respondents.[42] Other research suggests that "people typically offer more information in face-to-face interviews than in telephone interviews, . . . [and] telephone interviews obtain fewer comments in response to open-ended questions. . . . Otherwise, telephone interviews seem to obtain responses that are just as valid as and sometimes more valid than responses from face-to-face interviews."[43]

As noted above, almost all interviews were conducted privately with a single respondent. There is a danger that interviewing a respondent in front of an "audience" can affect his or her responses.[44] In three cases, respondents insisted that another member of their organization's staff be present during the interview. In two cases, this meant that the executive director wanted to participate along with the director of governmental affairs. In the third case, the volunteer chairman of the legislative committee and a paid staff member chose to respond together since they shared responsibility for the subject matter. Although it is impossible to assess whether the presence of an additional respondent affected the answers of the other individual, the respondents often engaged in active conversation and provided particularly detailed responses to the open-ended questions. In each of these cases, the additional person seems, on balance, to have improved the atmosphere of the interview.

As I will discuss in the next section, interviews consisted of both open- and closed-ended questions. Because of the nature of the open-ended questions and respondents' varying interest in participating in the study, interviews ranged from 35 to 150 minutes, with a median time of approximately 55 minutes.

In addition to writing the scaled responses directly onto the survey instrument during the interview and taking extensive notes on a legal pad, I also tape-recorded most of the interviews with the explicit permission of the respondents, allowing me to provide verbatim rather than approximate quotations in this book. Since most of the interviews were conducted under an implicit guarantee of anonymity, respondents are generally identified in the book text only by the type of organization they represent and their position within that organization.

Survey Instrument

The survey instrument consisted of approximately one hundred items (including follow-ups that are asked only under certain conditions). Quantitative data were collected for ninety-one variables in eight general categories:

- Interview parameters (identifying the domain and the specific interview)

- Organizational descriptors (providing descriptive information about the organization, the types of issues it deals with, and a series of items to plot the organization's ideological position)
- Organizational resources (measures of human and capital resources)
- Organizational links (connections to other organizations through current and former staff members, boards of directors, representatives, attorneys, and measures of perceived efficacy for the various links)
- Opinions on coalitions (views on formation, maintenance, and efficacy of coalitions)
- Importance of coalition activities (salience of various types of coalitions for the respondent)
- Coalition number and membership (participation in long-term coalitions, and membership of each)[45]
- Activities and coalition use (scaled responses regarding importance of twelve policy and political activities and coalition use in each)

A list of all variables appears in Appendix A, followed by the full text of the survey instrument.[46]

In addition to the quantitative/quantifiable data collected, groups were also asked to respond to a series of open-ended questions dealing with specific coalition experiences, their understanding of the manner in which coalitions were formed, coalition leadership, and cases when coalitions had proved impossible to form or maintain. These, along with unstructured responses, have proved extremely helpful in understanding the processes behind the relationships that appear in this book.

3

Choices, Benefits, and Brokers

INTRODUCTION

Coalitions play a more important role in the work of Washington representatives today than ever before.

> "Lobbying is no longer somebody coming with a bag full of money and laying it on a member's desk or relying on personal contacts to have the member do you a favor—if it ever was," explained Coretech lobbyist Stuart Eizenstat. "The difficulty of passing legislation has increased exponentially. To make a common cause with people who would not be your traditional allies is important."[1]

Despite the extensive collective action literature on the formation of interest groups, much less work has been done to explain coalitions of those groups. This is somewhat surprising, since a cursory glance through almost any account of how a bill became a law is likely to reveal a detailed description of the coalitions that supported or opposed the legislation. This chapter focuses on the incentives for and the character of an interest group's participation in policy coalitions, by which I mean purposive groups of organizations united behind a symbiotic set of legislative or regulatory goals.[2] I argue that the incentives a particular group responds to in joining a coalition strongly influence the ultimate role the group will play in the coalition structure.

In this chapter I examine several of the key reasons organizations participate in coalitions. Since Mancur Olson and Robert Salisbury wrote their seminal works on collective action and exchange theory, the collective action literature has stressed the provision of selective benefits by entrepreneurs to overcome the free-rider problem among

---

*An earlier version of this chapter appeared in Kevin Hula, "Rounding Up the Usual Suspects: Forging Interest Group Coalitions in Washington," in *Interest Group Politics*, 4th ed., ed. Allan J. Cigler and Burdett A. Loomis (Washington, D.C.: Congressional Quarterly Press, 1995), 239–58. The material is used with the permission of Congressional Quarterly Press.

groups pursuing collective goods.[3] I build upon their foundation, but with a proviso. Because of the nature of potential coalition members, the problems and incentives for collective action in political coalitions are somewhat different than the incentives offered by interest group entrepreneurs to overcome the free-rider problem.

INCENTIVES AND STRATEGY IN COALITION PARTICIPATION

Although it might seem intuitive that the groups involved in policy-oriented lobbying coalitions join primarily for strategic policy goals, a long literature on collective action suggests that this may not always be true.

Most of the collective action literature written since Mancur Olson's *The Logic of Collective Action* has focused on the origin and maintenance of interest groups, the free-rider problem, and the selective benefits offered by interest group entrepreneurs to potential members in exchange for their joining the organization. In its simplest form, the free-rider principle suggests that it is generally irrational for self-interested actors to expend resources to join a large group in pursuit of collective goods (such as clean air) unless they receive selective benefits as well. Because collective goods can be enjoyed by everyone whether or not they have contributed to the cause, the rational economic actor is expected to free ride, allowing others to pursue the goals in the political arena and enjoying the benefits nonetheless if they are forthcoming. Selective benefits have been considered generally in three broad categories: material, solidary, and expressive (or, alternatively, purposive).[4]

Does coalition formation among organizations represent the same collective action phenomenon as forming an interest group of individuals or firms? In many ways it does.[5] In other ways which I will suggest below, there are intriguing differences between forming coalitions and starting interest groups. Certainly we can observe similar incentives at work. Though there are innumerable reasons for an organization's Washington representative to join a political coalition, three stand out as particularly significant and will be discussed in this chapter. Sometimes organizations join coalitions for strategic reasons that might fall under what Peter B. Clark and James Q. Wilson would call "purposive" or Robert Salisbury would label "expressive." These strategic reasons deal with achieving a particular political goal. Sometimes they join for selective information benefits that they would not otherwise have had, primarily information or timely intelligence about the policy process. Still other groups join coalitions as a symbolic gesture—for example, to show their members that they are working actively on an issue or to demonstrate solidarity with another organization. I will argue that these groups are interested primarily in receiving symbolic benefits in return for this gesture. For any given coalition, there are probably members who have joined for each of these reasons.

The Free-Rider Question

Given the degree to which discussion of the free-rider problem dominates the literature on interest group formation, an obvious corollary arises in the study of collective action at the coalition level. Is it irrational for strategically minded groups not to free ride? In some cases, the fact that some organizations join coalitions to lobby for collective legislative goals can be explained partially by Olson's small-group principle: there are a limited number of potential coalition members for some issues, and in a small universe of organizations, the decision of a group to participate or not to participate can have a measurable impact on the political outcome of the issue. The motivation to free ride is reduced when nonparticipation measurably reduces the likelihood that the collective good will be achieved. Furthermore, the presence or absence of a given group is likely to be noticed in a small universe of organizations, and the potential exists for the application of coercive sanctions by other coalition members to discourage free riding. At the least, there may be a strong element of peer pressure.

However, there are more significant issues at stake, both theoretically and in practice, in explaining coalition formation. Relying on the small-group principle to explain collective action at the coalition level misses many of the unique characteristics observed in this form of collective action. Perhaps the most important distinction in the minds of the Washington representatives I interviewed is differences between the potential members of interest groups and the potential members of coalitions. The level of analysis in the study of coalition formation is the potential member. While the de jure potential member of a coalition is an organization, the de facto member of a coalition is a staff member who is employed by that organization to represent its interests in the legislative arena. This creates an important qualitative difference between the task confronting an interest group entrepreneur who must mobilize potentially apolitical individuals and the role of a coalition broker bringing paid Washington representatives into a coalition. In the first case, the free-rider problem grows from the potential member's reluctance to expend any resources for political action. In the second case, the representative who may well be politically active on that issue already is offered an opportunity to reduce his or her resource expenditure and increase the likelihood of policy success through a specific strategy, namely, a coalition. Already organized political interest groups are significantly different from the as-yet-uninvolved and therefore still unpolitical potential group members Olson describes. Because organized interests and their Washington representatives are *already* involved in the policy process, they have already crossed the act/do not act decision point. The question that these already mobilized groups face is the manner in which to act. For the group already mobilized to act, it may well be rational to join coalitions and share resources rather than to act alone as the sole resource expender. Thus, though Olson argues that individuals may join groups for positive selective benefits, organizational representatives in Washington often join coalitions to obtain policy goals at lower costs. Participation is clearly rational under these conditions.

Furthermore, the free-rider principle itself was developed to explain why individuals or organizations do not cooperate to achieve collective goods. However, most of the legislative goals pursued by coalitions are not pure collective goods. In fact, the issue is not only whether "the" policy will be enacted or defeated, but how the issue will be defined and what the distribution of benefits will be. As I will discuss later in this chapter, the rational group recognizes that opportunities to shape that policy in a unique fashion are often tied closely to membership in the coalition.

This is certainly not to imply that there are never free riders in the world of coalition politics. There are groups who may benefit from the work of a coalition without ever joining it. However, the more significant phenomenon among interest group lobbyists is more akin to what I would call "cheap riding" than "free riding." Some group leaders will lend their organization's name to a coalition's membership list or provide their nominal presence at coalition meetings in exchange for symbolic benefits. I discuss these peripheral coalition members with the term "tag-alongs" in chapter 4. For the present, I note merely that a theory of resource conservation would suggest that group leaders will expend the minimum effort necessary to achieve their legislative goals, but in a world of very, very imperfect political information the amount required to achieve these goals is murky at best.[6] Furthermore, even if a Washington representative's *legislative* goals could be met without lifting a finger, the "rational" representative might still become active in a coalition in order to obtain *professional* benefits.

Strategic Incentives for Participation

Some organizational leaders are motivated to participate in coalitions by strategic policy concerns. Given a range of political options, they select coalition strategies because they view them as the most effective way to shape policy outcomes. Although some organizations will always choose to be free riders, it is not necessarily irrational for

Washington representatives to join coalitions in pursuit of policy goals. Furthermore, from an institutional standpoint, politically active organizations have been pushed increasingly toward coalition strategy by developments in government and in the interest group system. In fact, the growth in the use of coalition strategies is a self-reinforcing phenomenon. As I will discuss below, the more organizations pursue coalition strategies, the more essential participation in coalitions may be to shaping favorable outcomes.

Institutional Imperatives

How do external, institutional conditions affect interest group strategies? Scholars such as Samuel Huntington, Hugh Heclo, and Daniel McCool have argued that such factors as the rapid growth in the number of interests represented in Washington, increasing policy complexity, and the increasing growth and decentralization of government have created an increasingly atomistic interest group system.[7] Burdett Loomis and William Browne have argued that the atomization of the interest group system has had the surprising effect of pushing groups *toward* coalition strategies.[8] Jeffrey Berry suggests that the coalition is, in fact, a form of conflict management that has grown in importance since the fall of subgovernments.[9] In my interviews, changes in government and the growth of organizational representation in Washington were the most frequently cited institutional explanations for coalition membership mentioned by organizations who join coalitions for strategic, legislative reasons.

Within the federal government, the number of institutional access points for organizations interested in a given policy has increased dramatically over the last twenty years. More members of Congress and their staffs have been brought into play at early stages of the legislative process as subcommittees have grown in number and as committees have expanded in jurisdiction through multiple referrals.[10] Organizations find it necessary to present their cases to more political actors than ever before.[11]

As former Reagan Chief of Staff Kenneth Duberstein noted, "It's not been like Lyndon Johnson's time, being able to work with 15 or 20 Congressmen and Senators to get something done. For most issues you have to lobby all 435 Congressmen and almost all 100 Senators."[12]

Duberstein's view was echoed by the director of government affairs at an agricultural organization:

> The way Congress does business has changed dramatically from the way it did business 20 or 30 years ago in a couple respects. Number one, in the old rigid seniority system, you tended to rely heavily on interpersonal

relationships between the representative of a particular industry and select [chairmen] in power. The legislature tended to have most of the power concentrated in their hands directly and not in the hands of staff. So if you cut a deal with that individual on your particular objective, it was done. . . . [But now] you have as many as five or six committees having jurisdiction over single issues—you have to deal not only with staff and the chairman but with other members on the committee before you can get a majority of the votes.

However, it is very difficult for even the largest individual groups to reach all the relevant congressional players, so collective strategies by similarly oriented organizations may be necessary if groups wish to present their cases in all the appropriate forums. A hallmark of coalition strategies is that membership enables the workload to be spread out. As Jeff Berry notes, "One interest group may have only two lobbyists; ten interest groups with the same number of lobbyists can provide twenty operatives for the coming battle."[13]

The second key institutional motivation for groups to join coalitions grows out of the explosive increase in the number of organizations active in Washington over the last three decades. As Jeff Berry, Jack Walker, Kay Schlozman and John Tierney, and Thomas Mann have pointed out, the number of public interest groups representing consumers, environmental concerns, and welfare interests expanded dramatically, as did the number of interest groups with foreign policy agendas and the number of business and trade associations active in Washington.[14] Today, the amazement E. Pendleton Herring recorded at the growth of group representatives by 1929 evokes an air of nostalgia: "At the present time a very conservative estimate places the total of these groups keeping representatives in the capital at well over five hundred. The writer has found the Washington addresses of five hundred and thirty. The telephone book alone lists over three hundred."[15]

Compare that with the situation in the late 1990s, when Ronald Shaiko counted over twenty-five hundred entries in the District of Columbia telephone directory that simply began with the words "National" or "American."[16] For Herring, the explanation for the rise of organized interest groups was "found in the decline of the political party as a leader in opinion."[17] Heclo argues that it occurred in large part because of governmental actions, noting the "almost inevitable tendency of successfully enacted policies unwittingly to propagate hybrid interests."[18] Whatever the cause, Salisbury has pointed out that the explosive growth in the number of organized interests since the 1960s has created a paradox: the creation of more groups has led to less clout for any of them.[19]

Lobbyists themselves are not unaware of this trend, and some cite it as a key reason why coalition strategies seem to be on the upswing. As one group representative pointed out, "I think coalitions can have a lot of value. Particularly today when there are so many voices from so many directions, I think coalitions are very important. And the list of them—they just seem to grow all the time."

As each new group is added to the Washington melee, governmental capacity to process external demands is reduced.[20] Raymond A. Bauer, Ithiel de Sola Pool, and Lewis Anthony Dexter argue that increasing demands upon members of Congress not only force them, but allow them, to pick and choose among the interests to which they will listen.

> [A] congressman's own decisions largely determine what pressures will be communicated to him. Paradoxical as it may seem, their "freedom" comes from the excessive demands made on them. The complexity of their environment which seems to congressmen to rob them of initiative thrusts initiative back on them, for, when the demands on a man's resources clearly exceed his capacity to respond, he *must* select the problems and pressures to which to respond.[21]

What kinds of problems and pressures do legislators prefer to avoid? The governmental affairs representative from a pipeline company noted that "members of Congress really hate to have to choose between people that they would like to have all as their friends, and if you go up as an industry and are divided, it's pretty difficult for them."

There is more pressure for groups to work out their differences outside the legislative process, rather than requiring Congress or the executive branch to sort out a seemingly infinite number of differences between groups. A lobbyist in a trucking-related industry noted that "coalitions are very effective because when members of Congress and their staff look at public policy issues, if they can avoid having to make some hard decisions because disparate industry groups have come to private resolution, it simplifies the official process."

In fact, committee chairs, congressional staffers, the Office of Public Liaison in the White House, and individual agencies all resort to initiating coalitions themselves, in order to encourage groups to work out what Douglas Costain and Anne Costain label "predigested policies" outside governmental institutions.[22] A trade association representative from the oil industry gave the example of the continual clashes between oil companies, oil jobbers, and service station dealers about wholesale and retail pricing: "Dingell was on the Energy and Commerce Committee. He says, 'Look, this is going on and on and on. If you people get together and talk about the industry—the oil companies and jobbers, and dealers—you guys get together and get it down what the problems are and see if you can't find some common ground and come back to us, and we will do something with it [then].'"[23]

When groups within an industry are unwilling or unable to work out differences and to present a united front to Congress, they may find Congress paralyzed. A trade association representative from the aircraft industry related how he and his colleagues became coalition organizers as a result of a complete breakdown in the system:

> Our interests are somewhat broader than the operators of the airplane, and we were able to kind of be the mediating force. Because we didn't have as many axes to grind, we could try to bring together a coalition rather than having everybody running around after themselves, which happened one year when the authorization and trust fund came up. We had all the different associations heading different directions and drawing for all kinds of radically different things. . . . Congress was [so] confused over what to do that they didn't pass the legislation. So we ended up for a short period of time where we had no authorization to fund the airport airway system. So I think we learned our lesson and the next year we tried to iron out our problems before we [went] up to Congress.

The growth in the number of interests represented in politics has been paralleled by an increasing public criticism of "special interest groups" over the last twenty years. Public and campaign rhetoric not only creates a more hostile political climate for organized interests, but it generates another reinforcing incentive for collective action. In order to avoid stigmatization as "special interest groups," individual organizations advocating particular policy outcomes turn to coalition strategies in an attempt to demonstrate diversity of support for their positions—in effect, seeking cover behind democratic rhetoric. A union leader stated:

> One other thing I would add . . . is that the more diverse you can make your coalition, the better. . . . [It looks like] good government—you know, broadly held ideals, a broad array of citizens with perceived wide varying interests, all interested on this issue. And that brings that issue into focus, so you've got more weight, and you sharpen that focus, and it's easier then with all that weight to push through the opposition.

This focus on public perception and on the rhetoric of public criticism is something different from a mere "weight in numbers" approach to politics. Broad coalitions create an aura of legitimacy.[24] Some coalitions are consciously structured to provide tactical cover for members of

Congress who fear being linked by the public to "special interest group politics:"

> [Being in a broad coalition] helps; yes, it does, especially with members of Congress. By and large, it's my perception . . . that the person on the street or the rank and file citizen is not into the coalition world, and "special interest" is viewed much differently than a *coalition* of so-called quote "special interests." (An educational association lobbyist)

Or, as the representative of a business association described his view of American democracy:

> [Y]ou get to sign a zillion names: all those members of the coalition who represent all those people in the organizations. You can go, say, on education, you're speaking for not just a hundred associations, but a hundred associations that represent every single facet of education from the janitors in the buildings to the principals to the supes to the school board members to the state superintendents to the governors. . . . And how that translates— I mean, guys up on the Hill aren't stupid. They know. But what they have to do is generate [a good story]—to find one day in the *Congressional Record* William Ford[25] saying, "A hundred zillion organizations and people all agree that Chapter I has to be increased" or "Head Start has to be increased." That plays well. It's a game, but it does the job. That's my feeling on the value of coalitions.

A related stigma-avoidance tactic is to form coalitions that will actually hide the participation of the coalition founder. This is particularly useful when an organization's overt participation in a lobbying effort seems either ineffective or counterproductive. When the California government ran aggressive antismoking advertisements funded through a tobacco tax, the Tobacco Institute developed a plan to quietly organize a coalition effort mobilizing citizens' groups within the black, Hispanic, and Asian communities as well as public health organizations. The coalition was to lobby the California state government to redirect the tax money spent on the media campaign to health care for the poor and other community-based programs. A senior vice president for the Tobacco Institute wrote, "Our goal is to keep the advertisements—not the tobacco industry—at the center of the controversy."[26]

Shaping the Issue Agenda from Within

One of the first stages of coalition formation is the development of an explicit policy goal around which groups can rally. Though the goal may be vague, such as preventing tax increases on airlines or supporting increased funding for education, it must be clear enough that organizations can identify themselves as being for or against it. This general policy goal is the common ground all organizations share, and in the early stages of that coalition, there is substantial flexibility around the edges as the members work toward a more rigorous self-definition. As the representative of a vocational organization pointed out, "What you want is a set of principles. You know, 'I will support any legislation that has the following principles in it.' And those principles are the driving issue. Otherwise you can't work out something that multiple organizations can support."

In the case of proactive coalitions—those that are formed to seek a change in the status quo—the general policy stance becomes more formalized as details are added and the edges of the coalition's platform are fleshed out. A large proactive coalition's platform often profoundly influences the terms of the ensuing policy debate; therefore, there is a strong incentive for sympathetic organizations to join the coalition in order to influence that platform with their own particular policy goals before the chorus begins to sing it in public. A teachers' union representative put it this way: "We prefer to be in the coalition early. When you see things forming, you want to be in it before the concrete sets."

The more inclusive the coalition, the more difficulty individual organizations outside the coalition have in shaping that issue. This is particularly true when the coalition contains divergent interests who are trying to work out differences outside the legislative arena and "precook" or "prepackage" a compromise position.[27] There is a powerful incentive to join coalitions in order to have a voice within them.

This is true even of coalitions ostensibly advocating collective goods. Collective, or "public," goods carry private as well as public benefits, and joining a coalition can be a strategy for seeking a favorable distribution of those benefits. It is, in part, a matter of perspective. Education funding, for example, is considered a collective good by the society at large. But for the representative of a school system, a college, a university, a research contractor, or any of the other organizations to whom the government funding is actually funneled, that funding quickly becomes a private good that someone else may be chosen to administer.

Take as an example the Committee for Education Funding (CEF), the best-known coalition in the education policy arena. CEF is a coalition of approximately one hundred organizations that lobbies for higher funding levels across the board for educational programs. Although education funding is hailed by the coalition as a public good, groups that join CEF do so not to guarantee overall education funding but to ensure that their particular programs are specifically included and explicitly advocated in CEF publications, lobbying, and testimony. By organizing and speaking with a common voice, CEF can define the public debate in terms of overall government funding on education while simultaneously making a case for each member's specific programs, in effect collectivizing the benefits and risks. A CEF member described the logic of the coalition this way:

> [CEF] is necessitated by our opponents who would take various organizations in the education arena and divide and conquer them, so to speak; in other words, put so much money on the table and say, "You [could] have this if X higher ed organization weren't also going after it." In other words, it would turn the education organizations against themselves. In order to get past that, we look at a full range of the kinds of funding needs that CEF members have, pool it all together, and we all go to bat for each other.

To state it mildly, CEF members are loath to think of losing the exposure their specific programs gain by virtue of their membership in the coalition.

Efficacy of Coalition Strategies

None of these policy-related incentives would be particularly important in the decision calculus of organizational leaders if they did not believe that coalitions were an effective solution for the institutional and issue-shaping challenges they faced. Charls Walker, known to many as the dean of the Washington lobbyists, has written that "Coalitions are the most important factors in getting a bill through Congress."[28] To systematically examine the opinions of Washington representatives toward coalitions, I presented respondents with an extensive series of statements regarding coalition membership and asked them to respond to each on a five point scale ranging from strong agreement to strong disagreement. Three of these statements dealt with efficacy, and the responses are recorded in table 3-1. Organizational representatives showed an overwhelming belief in the efficacy of coalitions for pursuing legislative goals.

Of all organizations from the transportation sample, 81.3 percent agreed to the statement "Coalitions are the way to be effective in politics." Slightly less, 79.6 percent of the education sample, agreed, and slightly more, 83.3 percent of the civil rights sample, agreed. Only 8.4 percent of the transportation sample, and 4 percent of the education sample disagreed. No groups in the civil rights sample disagreed.

The statement "Being a member of a coalition helps an organization to control the outcome of an issue" elicited agreement from 75 percent of the transportation respondents, 77.6 percent from the education respondents, and 83.3 percent of the civil rights sample. Disagreement rates were 16.7 percent, 10.2 percent, and 6.6 percent for transportation, education, and civil rights, respectively, with the remaining groups in each sample neither agreeing nor disagreeing.

TABLE 3-1
Coalition Efficacy
(By Percentage Responding)

		Cumulative Agree	Agree Strongly	Agree Somewhat	Neither	Disagree Somewhat	Disagree Strongly	N
Coalitions are the way to be effective in politics.	Transportation	81.3	43.8	37.5	10.4	6.3	2.1	(48)
	Education	79.6	38.8	40.8	16.3	2.0	2.0	(49)
	Civil Rights	83.3	50.0	33.3	16.7	0.0	0.0	(30)
Being a member of a coalition helps an organization to control the outcome of an issue.	Transportation	75.0	35.4	39.6	8.3	14.6	2.1	(48)
	Education	77.6	24.5	53.1	12.2	8.2	2.0	(49)
	Civil Rights	83.3	23.3	60.0	10.0	3.3	3.3	(30)
If our organization does not join a coalition, we may lose our ability to shape the outcome of the issue.	Transportation	55.5	11.1	44.4	6.7	31.1	6.7	(45)
	Education	40.8	12.2	28.6	20.4	28.6	10.2	(49)
	Civil Rights	63.3	26.7	36.7	13.3	23.3	0.0	(30)

Note: Some rows may not sum to 100 due to rounding.

Responses were somewhat more balanced when organizational representatives were presented with the statement "If our organization does not join a coalition, we may lose our ability to shape the outcome of the issue." Fifty-five point five percent of the transportation groups, 40.8 percent of the education groups, and 63.3 percent of the civil rights groups agreed. Disagreement came from 37.8 percent of the respondents from transportation, 38.8 percent of the education sample, and 23.3 percent of the civil rights groups. The balance, again, neither agreed nor disagreed.[29]

Though these responses do not show why particular groups join particular coalitions, they do demonstrate an overwhelming sense of efficacy in coalition strategies across the board in three policy spheres.[30] In fact, a majority of the organizations active in the transportation and civil rights policy domains and a plurality of organizations active in the education domain feel that they may in fact be incapable of shaping an issue if they do not join a coalition.

Information as a Selective Benefit

In coalitions, as in the case of interest groups, there are a number of membership incentives that are not directly related to pursuing specific public policy goals. For those groups not joining political coalitions for purposive reasons, information is the single most important selective benefit. Information is a difficult benefit to categorize. In some cases it appears to be a material benefit with monetary value. At other times the information exchange is laden with solidary benefits. What is clear, however, is that joining coalitions for information is a common phenomenon. This is not surprising, in view of the research done by Salisbury and colleagues, by Edward Laumann and David Knoke, and by John Heinz et al., demonstrating the importance of information gathering and communications among Washington group representatives.[31]

There are many types of information, some more difficult to obtain than others.[32] Interest group entrepreneurs want to know about upcoming threats to their organizations' perceived interests. This type of information may come, for example, in the form of a "heads up" warning before legislation is introduced, notice that a coalition is forming to pursue a goal antithetical to the organization's own agenda, or a tip that a journalist is working on a story that may paint the organization in an unflattering light.

Washington representatives are particularly interested in getting the latest updates on a bill's content and status in the legislative process. Information about possible amendments and likely head counts is essential to effective lobbying, and coalitions are a means of obtaining this information efficiently. However, information is not equally important across groups as an incentive for participation in strategic policy coalitions. Information benefits are particularly important as incentives for smaller groups with limited staff and resources. For organizations with only one staff member assigned to government relations, simply keeping up with the daily publications describing government activities can take up a significant portion of that representative's day. As one overworked staff member representing school officials noted, "if you are not a part of the loop, it shuts you out of things you may need to be aware of. And there's so much to know. There's no way you can keep up with just the *Federal Register* and the *Congressional Record* unless you have a big staff or a lot of lawyers."

This lobbyist's situation is not unique. In fact, one-third of the organizations active in either the transportation or the education domain had only one professional with governmental relations duties on staff. In several cases that person also served as executive director. A full 55 percent of the transportation sample and 50 percent of the education sample had two or fewer professionals assigned to government relations. By contrast, groups active in the civil rights domain tended to have more government relations staffers: 77 percent of these groups interviewed had more than two government relations staffers.

In addition to following the introduction of bills and proposed regulations, small staffs without significant contacts on the Hill may find it nearly impossible to keep track of activities in the relevant subcommittees, follow legislation between hearings and markups, and keep in contact with relevant congressional staff. For these groups, coalitions are a lifeline of information, scuttlebutt, and rumors about developments in the policy process. Coalition partners may function as an early warning system for developing issues that a representative had not been following.

> It's very important [to be in a coalition], because people tend to talk about things that I might only have a tangential interest in or might not think is important, and it's very important for information sharing. Saves you about a dozen phone calls when you can have a regular meeting where people can bring those kinds of things to the table. (A lobbyist for an educational discipline)

Group Maintenance and the Symbolic Benefits of Coalition Membership

The interest group leaders who were interviewed noted frequently that a key component of group maintenance is showing their membership that the Washington staff is busy. Photographs of organizational leaders testifying before a congressional committee or subcommittee frequently grace the first page of group newsletters. Some group leaders view participation in a coalition as a low-cost trophy that they can deliver to their membership to demonstrate activity on issues which group leaders view as secondary, if not downright unimportant. The investment is small—perhaps only attending an hour-long meeting each month. This phenomenon is not restricted to membership associations. A Washington corporate representative in the trucking industry noted that she sometimes joins coalitions ". . . [b]ecause it's seen as the thing to do, perhaps by corporate headquarters. *They* may say, 'This is an issue that's important to us.' But *we* [in Washington] can't spend a lot of time on it, so we're going to give it nominal support. We want to show [headquarters] that this is an 'important' issue." Corporate lobbyists are sometimes instructed by headquarters to be active on issues, whether or not there is a window of opportunity.[33] Participating in a coalition may demonstrate activity, even when the representatives do not expect a positive policy return.

In essence, joining a coalition as a purely symbolic action can satisfy group members or a corporate hierarchy because of a principal-agent problem.[34] Most group members and many corporate executives located outside Washington do not have the political experience and information necessary to adequately interpret and supervise the activities of their Washington representatives. For the Washington representatives, corporate misconceptions about the legislative process can be a frustrating burden, as was the case with this former auto industry lobbyist who stressed that Detroit was out of touch with the political realities of Washington:

> There is a certain mentality within a corporation that says "Lay out our objective for the year." It's very difficult to do that in a political environment. . . . [T]hey were used to goals, you know, by the end of the month you're gonna have this done. You're gonna have this. You know how many hours it takes to produce a car. You have a timeline. Or you've got production goals for the year. Congress doesn't work like that. . . . And that's what a lot of times in the private sector people lose sight of when they're trying to do government relations. . . . You can demand something when you're in a corporation; you can set goals, and you can fire people. Congress doesn't work that way, and government doesn't work that way, really. [Corporations] don't understand the fluid element that's involved.

The decision organizational representatives make to participate symbolically in a strategic coalition rather than to lobby actively on an issue amounts to a sophisticated form of "shirking," to borrow a term from principal-agent theory.

Claiming credit for symbolic participation in coalitions occurs not only in large coalitions but in small activities such as joint letter signing. The extreme form of this symbolic activity can be seen in cases where groups volunteer to sign onto joint projects or letters without knowing the substantive content. The director of government affairs for a relatively arcane branch of higher education related this example:

> One of the other associations knows that [Rep.] Ford wants the Hawkins-Stafford recommendations. So he called me and said, "Are you doing this?" I said, "Yes, I'm doing it." And he said, "Can I sign on?" I mean, he doesn't even know what I'm doing, but he doesn't want to spend the time doing it, because it's not important to him, but he wants to be part of the game. So he called and said "I assume you're doing this. Unless it's something that we can't live with, I want to just tell you I will sign on to what you're going to recommend." Two other associations have done that as well. So there are three that just out of the blue called me, and it's because no one else does this, really.

Why did these groups want to sign on? Rather than signing on to the letter because of substantive policy goals, they were signing for the sake of an audience—so they could tell their members that they had worked on the project and could show the relevant committee staff that they were active in the policy area. Symbolic participation also occurs in cases where an organization joins a coalition for reasons such as paying back a debt, doing a favor for another group, or setting an example for other organizations.

Clearly, groups join coalitions for a number of different reasons, some of them apparently only tangentially related to strategic public policy goals. The results of this asymmetry in the goals of coalition members will be examined in the next chapter.

CONCLUSION

The literature on collective action has focused on the provision of selective benefits to potential members in exchange for their participation in a group. In this chapter I have examined the role of selective benefits in a particular type of collective action—political coalitions. I have suggested that the benefits sought by organizations joining a coalition are generally similar to those sought by individuals joining a group, though there are some key differences.

Given the emphasis that group theorists place on the free-rider problem, it is worth recapping why I downplay that problem in this chapter on coalition formation. There is an important difference between the free-rider problem that group entrepreneurs face when trying to mobilize potential group members and the challenge facing a coalition broker trying to harmonize the activities of professional Washington representatives. The heart of the free-rider problem for a group entrepreneur is to convince potentially uninvolved individuals that they should get involved in an issue by offering them a package of selective benefits that they can receive only if they join the group. Coalition brokers operate in a different environment, however, in which professional Washington representatives keep their jobs and seek promotion by keeping abreast of issues important to their employer and demonstrating their effective involvement in those political issues. The task for the coalition broker is not to provide incentives for people to get involved on an issue, but rather to convince these already active Washington representatives that they could be more effective at what they are already doing by pursuing their goals in cooperation with other Washington representatives. The incentives relevant to coalition members are tailored to their profession as lobbyists.

Strategically motivated Washington representatives perceive coalitions as an efficacious strategy for influencing public policy. By helping organizations to pool resources in pursuit of a common legislative goal, coalitions help strategically minded organizations to face the challenges brought on by institutional changes in the government and in the increasingly complicated interest group universe.

Not all coalition members are motivated by strategic policy concerns. Washington representatives from some organizations join political coalitions primarily to receive selective benefits such as information and intelligence, or to demonstrate symbolic action to their membership or their corporate superiors. These symbolic benefits enable organizational representatives to shirk, in the language of principal-agent theory.

Obviously, every group representative does not join every coalition into which he or she is invited, but the tendency to ascribe this immediately to the free-rider problem should be resisted. Groups that simply stay out of the coalition may have no interest in the legislation (these are not free riders), or they may be pursuing their own strategy outside the coalition (these are not free riders), or it is possible that they are in fact true free riders who hope to benefit from the coalition's work without lifting a finger. However, since the level of analysis is the paid, professional Washington representative, if the legislative issue is high on his or her group's priority list, there are strong incentives for that person not to be a true free rider and gamble that others will bring home the bacon.

Incentive theory is useful to explain not only why groups join a coalition but also what roles they will play in the coalition once they are members.

4

Core Members, Players, and Tag-alongs: Incentives and Coalition Structure

INTRODUCTION

In this chapter I argue that the incentives a particular group responds to in joining a coalition strongly influence the ultimate role the group will play in the coalition structure. Understanding whether a group joins a coalition for *strategic reasons* or *selective benefits*, discussed in chapter 3, also helps determine whether it will become a "core member," a "player," or a "peripheral member" of that coalition. At the aggregate level, the distribution of goals, priorities, and resources across coalition members determines the coalition's organizational structure.

COALITION STRUCTURE AND MEMBERSHIP ASYMMETRY

A group's incentive preferences affect not only its decision to participate but also its ultimate position and role in a coalition. When one examines specific coalitions, it is quickly apparent that different groups shoulder different amounts of responsibility. This is closely correlated to the reasons these groups joined the coalition. Put simply, the position a group holds in a coalition and the role it plays is determined by the confluence of a group's goals, priorities, and resources.

Coalition members can be divided roughly into three concentric groups: coalition core groups, coalition players, and peripheral groups (see figure 4-1).

---

*An earlier version of this chapter appeared in Kevin Hula, "Rounding Up the Usual Suspects: Forging Interest Group Coalitions in Washington," in *Interest Group Politics*, 4th ed., ed. Allan J. Cigler and Burdett A. Loomis (Washington, D.C.: Congressional Quarterly Press, 1995), 239–58. The material is used with the permission of Congressional Quarterly Press.

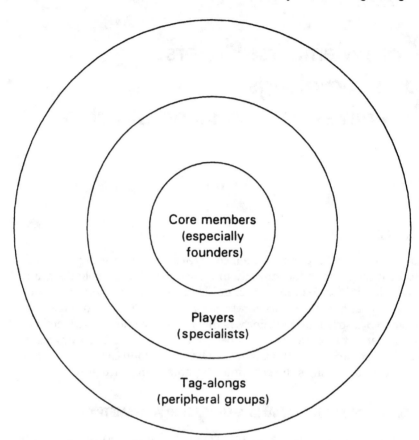

Figure 4-1. Coalition Membership and Structure

The *coalition core* is made up primarily of the founders and other resource-rich groups who join the coalition to achieve broad strategic policy goals. Core members are notable for their willingness to expend high levels of resources to promote overall legislative victory. The members of the ring closest to the core can be thought of as *players*. Players tend to be specialists who join a coalition for tactical reasons; these groups are highly interested in shaping specific provisions of the legislation in question. They are characterized by their desire to hone the issues. Players are willing to spend a fairly high level of resources in order to achieve their specific policy goals. The third group of members consists of *peripheral groups* who tend to tag-along with the rest of the coalition for nonpolicy incentives such as information or group maintenance benefits. While generally supportive of coalition goals, these groups are not willing to expend significant resources for a coalition victory. Rather, membership in the coalition is an end in itself.

A summary of these relationships between coalition members, their goals, resources, and coalition positions is shown in table 4-1.

The asymmetry in organizational goals and resources that groups bring to a coalition has practical implications. The distribution of goals and resources across groups in a coalition determines the structure of that coalition. This point bears closer examination.

The Core Groups

Core members and players both believe that they can affect policy outcomes, and they join the coalition to achieve policy goals. Both sets of members have a sense of efficacy, but it manifests itself differently for each set. Core members are intent on final legislative outcomes and a broader strategic approach to those outcomes. This is certainly the case for the founding members, who must be willing to finance the bulk of the coalition's expenses in the early stages. Coalition founders, or brokers, to use Burdett Loomis's term, are at the heart of the core group.[1]

TABLE 4-1.
Coalition Members, Their Goals, and Their Resources

	Core Member	Specialist, or Player	Peripheral or Tag-along
Issue importance	High (broad)	High (specific)	Low (peripheral)
Organization's goal	Overall strategic victory	Issue honing	Coalition by-products
Degree and type of resources brought by an organization	High level of: • time • money • reputation • expertise • membership	Enough to buy a place at the negotiating table: • expertise • reputation • membership • money	Only their name: • perhaps a prestigious name • perhaps just another name for the list
Time commitment (work level)	High level for overall goal	High level for specific goals	Low level across the board

As Loomis points out, coalitions do not simply emerge. Rather, they are assembled by an individual or small group of individuals who play a role more similar to that of a broker than to that of a group entrepreneur. The broker provides the initial stimulus and capital to organize the coalition. At a minimum this includes hosting the coalition, chairing or co-chairing the coalition, and providing clerical support for organizational tasks. Founders want more groups to join their coalitions for strategic reasons; they believe coalition size and diversity increase the likelihood of eventual policy success. Because of the critical role coalition brokers play in organizing a coalition, they are likely to play a continuing, core role in coalition leadership for some time. Although the use of attorneys, public relations firms, and other professional coalition brokers to start coalitions has grown in recent years (Anne Wexler is perhaps the best-known example), most cooperative lobbying efforts among groups are started by organizational staff lobbyists.

In many cases, the coalition is managed by its members, and no financial transactions occur. In other cases, an external coalition staff may be hired after the fact to coordinate ongoing coalition activities. However, these individuals should not be confused with the founders, though they are core actors. As the director of government relations for an agricultural organization noted, sometimes groups

> look to share the costs both in terms of real dollar costs and the hiring of outside counsel. Or, sometimes you will hire a lobbyist. It may be an attorney, a lobbyist in an attorney's clothing, where you'll hire somebody that will sort of spend full-time while all the other individuals are part-time on that issue to provide the continuity and the in-depth work if necessary to be successful. . . . Sometimes one organization cares a whole lot more than someone else so they themselves will provide that continuity, but there are some issues where they're so cross-cutting, there's no single organization that really has it as his top priority—uh, so you hire somebody.
>
> We're in a coalition called the Minor Crop Farmer Alliance—it has to do with when to use pesticides. That in and of itself is a very important issue, but for any single organization, not at the top of its hit list, and, so we needed somebody with technical expertise, legal expertise, and the Hill type of expertise just to sort of provide the bonding cement of the individual players. And so, you know, twenty organizations basically get together and each chips some money in, and, uh, the law firm that we hired provides . . . continuity and some of the contacts and then we all chip in with our individual capabilities off and on, as the need arises or as we have the time.

In general, coalitions are initiated more frequently by large organizations than by small organizations and, not surprisingly, more frequently by groups with a strong, broad interest in a particular legislative issue within their policy domain than by groups outside that domain with a secondary interest in that issue. Reputation, centrality of the issue to the group's self-identification, and political resources all weigh heavily in enhancing the likelihood that a given organization can successfully found a coalition.

Core membership is not restricted solely to the brokers of a coalition. Other groups may become core members of the coalition if they have a strong commitment to the overall coalition goal and are willing to devote time, energy, and other resources to coalition work. Because of their size, reputation, and resources, some groups are almost automatic core members if they choose to voice a strong opinion within the coalition. A representative from one of the two major teachers' unions noted, "We try not to [dominate coalitions], *try* not to, especially try not to foster or feed that kind of thing. But, by and large, in many coalitions, if we are opposed to something, it may influence. If we're for something it may influence others."

In his "Second Discourse on Inequality," Jean-Jacques Rousseau lays out an important collective action problem relevant to this discussion when he describes the challenges facing primitive people hunting a stag:

> If a Deer was to be caught, everyone clearly sensed that this required him faithfully to keep his post; but if a hare happened to pass within reach of one of them, he will undoubtedly have chased after it without a scruple and, having caught his own prey, have cared very little about having caused his Companions to miss theirs.[2]

Kenneth Waltz reintroduced Rousseau's parable into modern discourse through his analysis of this collective action problem among states in the international arena. In Waltz's work, the challenge of pursuing mutual interests over a sustained period under the condition of international anarchy is generally insurmountable.[3] However, in the case of interest group coalitions, core members are united by specific policy goals. Mutual interests are defined in terms of legislation. In Rousseau's framework, to which I will soon return, one could say that core members simply will settle for nothing less than a stag. Not all tastes are negotiable.

In many coalitions the core is defined explicitly for functional reasons. If a coalition becomes too large and diverse for consensual agenda setting and logistical control, core members create a leadership committee to carry out these functions. As the director of governmental relations for a children's lobby put it,

[You need to] form a nucleus of your coalition. The Children First coalition has got some sixty groups in it. Well, that's too big to plan the agenda. But we're trying right now to [form] what we call sort of an executive committee, or, you know a working group, that will meet more often than the larger group, talk about some issues, and spread the work out too. So we're trying to again pull in the education and business leaders and groups here into that so we can get the word out, get interesting agendas, and then share in the responsibilities of putting together a program.

Players: The Specialists

Like core members, players also join coalitions to pursue policy goals. They, too, are interested in achieving eventual policy successes, but they may have more limited goals. Because a proactive coalition's position may strongly influence the terms of debate on an issue, it is important for strategically motivated groups with specialized but related interests to seek inclusion of their interests in the coalition's platform. Without membership in the coalition, they have little ability to shape the policy position of that coalition.

Although players tend to be interested in or affected by a smaller portion of the legislation in question than core members, they bring a specialized expertise to the coalition that the core members may lack. This expertise on specific points of the legislation is their key source of political capital within the coalition. Because players may not hold great sway in the overall legislative battle as individual groups, their narrow focus and expertise are used primarily in shaping the coalition's agenda and honing the coalition's position on the points that are relevant to them. When asked whether their membership really made any difference in a coalition, the manager of federal affairs for a professional association said:

> In terms of *what the coalition is saying* to the Hill or the administration, then I would say yes. One can be effective within the coalition without necessarily being able to judge how effective the coalition is in the overall outcome of the issue. Being a member of the coalition can help you to shape the position of a coalition.

None of this is to suggest that players do not expend resources outside the coalition. They do. However, their lobbying efforts in the legislative arena, as within the coalition, tend to be focused on their specific piece of the issue or legislation rather than the package as a whole.

A player's likelihood to join a coalition is based upon the perception that he can piggyback his proposal onto the coalition platform. But piggybackers are in many ways like the participants in the stag hunt. Returning to Rousseau's stag hunt, if players can catch their little rabbit alone, they are unlikely to join the stag hunt in the first place, let alone continue the hunt after they have caught their own dinner on the side. Given the nature of the policy process, players in defensive coalitions trying to stop a specific provision contained in a piece of legislation are more likely to defect than players who have joined a proactive coalition in pursuit of passage. It is almost axiomatic that it is easier to kill a piece of legislation than it is to pass one. This applies to specific provisions as well. If a player in a defensive coalition succeeds in getting a provision dropped from a bill, that player may become a peripheral member of the coalition or drop out entirely. On the other hand, a player in a proactive coalition generally does not have the luxury of dropping out until the bill is signed or the provision is killed. Players who remain in the coalition perceive that their specific goals are linked to the overall success of that coalition.

The converse to this provides a potential strategy for an opposing coalition. If players in a proactive coalition can be convinced that their provisions are more likely to be passed as part of a different piece of legislation, the opposition may be able to buy them off and weaken the coalition. In this case, "compromise and negotiation" with individual coalition members paradoxically can be a strategy to defeat the overall goal of the coalition.

Salisbury and his colleagues reported that primary intergroup relationships are found within the same policy sphere and are, furthermore, frequently among groups that are functionally most similar.[4] It follows that founders and other core members are generally from within the same policy domain, while players or specialists may come from other domains. Furthermore, organizations that are core members of one coalition are likely to be core members of other coalitions in that issue domain.

When shown a draft of figure 4-1, the manager of federal relations for a professional association of scientists confirmed these general observations and pointed out important differences among specialists, hired outside lobbyists, and core members in long-term coalitions:

[The specialists are involved] just to make sure their view was taken into consideration when this group was developing its position. I find in my experience these people would tend to be more the folks that are the lobbyists-for-hire types, the folks that have specific clients—not part of an association or a society, but are, you know, they've got multiple clients with multiple interests. . . . Now sometimes they're in here if it's something that's very fundamental to their interests. . . . But they don't tend to be in this long-term core. . . . I mean we [in the core] have a long-term concern about these issues, not just exactly what is the funding in this particular year. Because our jobs in associations like mine—I don't lose my job if NSF doesn't get its requested amount of funding next year, or I don't lose my job if I can't come through with a congressman on a key vote, whereas somebody like this does. Because they are on a case-by-case basis. They have a contract. We have the luxury, if you will, of taking a longer-term view and a bigger-picture view.

In fact, if players are unable to integrate or to piggyback their particular interests into the broader coalition platform, they are likely to leave the coalition.

Peripheral Groups: The Tag-Alongs

Peripheral groups, or "tag-alongs," are in some respects the most interesting types of coalition members. These are the coalition members that have neither a compelling commitment to the legislation in question nor a willingness to expend significant efforts to achieve the eventual policy goal that serves as the focus of the coalition. Yet these groups join to receive selective benefits available in the coalition such as information or the benefits of symbolic participation for their members.

An example brought up by the leader of a trade organization representing one segment of the auto service and repair industry demonstrates the links between minimal involvement, peripheral membership in a coalition, and symbolic benefits to present to the group's membership.

You can't take the lead on everything. But you can be part of it . . . let [other groups] take the lead and give them support and meet with them so you know what's going on. A real good example of it right now—House Bill 1790—Gephart's bill. Kind of a knockoff-parts bill—it looks like it. What it seemed to be doing is to prevent people from making after-market parts. And our industry here . . . that's what most of us deal with is after-market parts. And [they are] frequently better than the original equipment. They are trying to prevent the knockoffs from Korea and Japan and all that, but it was an issue that was important to some of our people, but not nearly as important to us as it was to the parts manufacturers and the parts distributors, and they really got involved in it. . . . They took the lead for us, but we attended all the coalition meetings. We knew what was going on. And when we got jumped on at our [own trade association's] meeting, about "What the hell—you are not doing anything about this!" [we could respond,] "Yes, we are. We know exactly where it is, and they [parts manufacturers and distributors] are taking the lead."

Returning to the story of Rousseau's stag hunt, we can view tag-alongs as a third group in the woods. Unlike the hunters, who are actively pursuing the stag, peripheral groups are not really planning to exert themselves beyond walking into the woods. They are just tagging along in case the rest of the group gets the big one, in which case they can share in the credit since they were there when the stag was felled. Though not complete free riders, peripheral groups are certainly discount hunters.

This does not escape the attention of core members. A senior manager at an industrial trade association explained:

> I would say that maybe 10 percent of them do [the work]. The rest of them are just there for information gathering. . . . Just because someone joins a coalition doesn't mean they're going to do much. A lot of them just do it for information, or, you know, someone at their company [says] "Oh, you have to get involved in this issue." Well, okay, I'm "involved"— I went to a coalition meeting.

Peripheral groups are not necessarily resource-poor or apolitical. Even the largest politically active organizations function in a peripheral capacity on some issues. Because of the reputation, resources, and perceived clout of some organizations within an issue domain, coalition brokers see their membership, even if inactive, as critical to the success of the coalition. Particularly on obscure issues in which the desired organization might not be interested, the broker's job becomes much more difficult.

> I can occasionally drag along the NEA, and I can occasionally drag along one of the [school] principals' organizations, but it really is not the main focus for them, and so, because it is not of great interest to them, one of two things happens. They either say, "Oh . . . I just can't be bothered with it" or they say, "All right, as a favor, use our name on the letter with you." But it's more a courtesy than getting them involved and having them marshal their memberships, along with marshaling our membership, because it's my issue, and they don't see it so much as their issue.

A lobbyist for one of the two major teachers' unions described the other side of the relationship somewhat smugly: "The perception is that if we're not going to play, that it will affect the outcome. We are sought after to be on coalitions." Where smaller organizations may seek inclusion in coalitions as peripheral members for benefits such as information, the big guns of an issue domain do not respond to those incentives. They are themselves probably the best sources of intelligence in a coalition and do not need to seek inclusion in a coalition for that type of benefit. In cases like the one above, the peripheral group lends its name to the coalition as a favor, but active participation will not be forthcoming.

INTERACTION AMONG MEMBERS

As noted above, coalition members bring very different goals, levels of interest, and resources to a coalition, and yet the asymmetries in coalition membership are generally acceptable to all the organizations because an exchange is taking place. On the one hand, the coalition has the benefit of a group's name to present to Congress and can claim additional diversity in the coalition's membership. As a health and education lobbyist noted, "Some [of the coalition members] are not even headquartered here, so they kind of keep in touch by mail. But they're also very effective as a name to lend to a list. If you have three hundred associations on a list, that's a pretty strong message."

On the other hand, the member organization, even if inactive in the legislative arena, has gained a source of information or a symbolic activity trophy to hold up before its membership. Furthermore, the group may have developed contacts and potential allies for higher-priority issues in the future.

In several of my interviews, respondents noted the importance of coalition leaders' being able to differentiate between groups that were willing to work for the policy goals and groups that were just "warming seats"—that is, the real players and the peripheral groups.

> You know, some people belong to larger coalitions because they want to learn something, and have some information to carry forward. Others will give you their time and effort on Capitol Hill. I think you have to look at both of those. . . . And then you have to evaluate who's in there for the "yeah, this is gonna be a high priority for me too" or "I'm in here because it's a medium or low priority for me, and I just want to make sure that I'm up on the issues" (A medical association lobbyist)

Yet not a single group leader suggested that the tag-alongs were not welcome in the coalition. Whereas some coalitions require a monetary contribution to join, other coalitions have no fee structure at all, and intriguingly, fee-based coalitions occasionally waive the required monetary contribution completely for groups with fewer resources in order to present a larger membership list to legislators. Though the tag-along's contribution might have been merely to add another signature to joint letters, that was in itself a welcome addition. This may be particularly important for defensive coalitions that form to oppose legislation. John Heinz and his colleagues note from their survey data that the number of organizations opposing a legislative proposal has a statistically significant (inverse) relationship ($p<.005$) with the likelihood that a proposal will succeed.[5]

Some respondents who would see themselves as core members of coalitions expressed frustration that more groups were not willing to commit more time and energy to the coalition's broad legislative goals, but even these groups did not suggest that the peripheral groups be expelled. On another issue, they might be peripheral groups themselves. In spite of the asymmetry in the goals of core members, players, and peripheral members, there is a symbiotic relationship. Each organization is welcome to whatever benefit that group joins to receive, so long as it does not infringe on the legislative interests of other coalition members.

Acrimony, however, can develop if tag-alongs shade their real intentions or misrepresent the position of their membership. Consider the case of California's Proposition 187. Looking back on the 1994 passage of the bill aimed at illegal aliens, the former vice president of the Mexican American Legal Defense and Education Fund (MALDEF) expressed a sense of betrayal:

> The coalition assembled to defeat Proposition 187 was impressive; it was extraordinarily broad. It was also extraordinarily shallow. Every sector of the California population was officially opposed to this measure. Organizations representing senior citizens, children, civil rights, women, law enforcement, educators, health care professionals, labor, even environmentalists all were on record as opposing Proposition 187. But on election day, it was the organizations in name only that opposed the measure, and not their constituents. With a few notable exceptions, a majority of virtually every demographic group voted for the measure.[6]

Although core members of the coalition against Proposition 187 were caught off guard when the tag-alongs did not deliver the votes, students of E. E. Schattschneider will recognize the law of "imperfect political mobilization" at work.[7] A frequent broker of coalitions in the education field noted that in forming and maintaining a coalition, he dealt with several different kinds of groups, including

> those organizations that we know pretty well can deliver; those organizations that talk a good game but don't deliver; those that can count votes; those that influence votes; and those that think they can, but can't. I guess you really learn to separate the real deliverers from those who want to be deliverers—and in a coalition, try not to shut down any of them.

Not shutting down any of them means not cutting off the flow of coalition membership incentives to any of the members, lest they defect.

CONCLUSION

In this chapter I have suggested that incentive theory is useful not only to explain why groups join a coalition but also to explain the roles they will play in the coalition once they are members. In fact, the goals, priorities, and resources that an organization brings to the coalition will determine the ultimate role the group will play in that coalition.

Groups who join a coalition for broad strategic goals are generally willing to commit time and effort to carrying the coalition's platform into battle. They are the core members, the leaders of the coalition. Organizations which join coalitions for more narrow strategic goals are unlikely to become core members, but these specialists are still players in the coalition. Because of their more narrow priorities, they focus their work within the coalition on tactically shaping the coalition platform to include their particular interest. Their external lobbying on behalf of the coalition focuses on their slice of the coalition platform as well. These specialists are willing to commit time and resources to the coalition to the degree that it continues to include their particular goal. Organizations that join a coalition for symbolic reasons or solely in order to gain benefits such as information are generally unwilling to expend significant resources to further the coalition goal. Though they support the goal in principle, coalition membership is an end in itself, and they will remain on the periphery of the coalition.

The heart of the exchange brokered in coalitions is that groups contribute whatever they are willing to, and this donation is tied to what they want to get out of the coalition. If a group representative wants to be a coalition leader, he or she cannot merely donate his or her name to a list but must provide substantial time and resources. On the other hand, if the only thing the representatives want is to get a paragraph for their newsletter or to pay back a debt, they will merely contribute their names. Peripheral groups are not free riding, though, because all the groups in the coalition have entered into a transaction, and the other participants in the coalition have agreed to the legitimacy of the exchange.

5

Looking for Partners: Information, Structural Links, and the Problem of Coordination

INTRODUCTION

Though lobbying coalitions are a popular strategy among Washington representatives, they do not form by themselves. In fact, before a coalition broker can begin pulling groups together, he or she faces an information challenge. An interest group leader who wishes to develop a cooperative relationship with other organizations on a given issue must first ascertain the interests and preferences of other groups in the Washington environment. Although Washington lobbyists and group representatives may be better versed than the man on the street in the nature of the policy process and the preferences of political actors, they do not operate with perfect and complete information. When they are presented with a policy concept or a legislative initiative, the information challenge is twofold. First, group leaders must identify the other organizations that might be interested in the policy; second, they must determine the policy preferences of these potentially interested organizations.

Though I do not wish to overstate the role of information or the difficulty of finding members for a coalition, it is important to recognize the significance of this preliminary stage for coordinating political action. Groups need information before they can mobilize jointly.

Individuals and organizations that already have this information about potential coalition partners and foes (or can ascertain the information quickly at a low cost) have an obvious advantage, a proverbial leg up, in their ability to broker a coalition. Where links between institutions overcome the information problem, organizations achieve collective action more readily. We will discuss each of these questions at length below. I will return to this topic in chapter 6 to explore how changes in technology affect these information questions.

As Robert Salisbury has pointed out, the most time consuming interest group activities are generally related to intelligence gathering rather than direct lobbying.[1] This insight is the starting point for understanding the informational challenges of political coordination between interest groups.

Is Anybody Out There? Identifying Interested Parties

Organizational representatives cannot coordinate political action with other groups until they know which organizations are interested and ready to participate in the issue at hand. This amounts to identifying the potential set of political players on an issue, an information challenge that can be larger for some groups than for others.

In the prelegislative stages of agenda formation, policy concepts are general, fluid, and abstract. As John Kingdon has argued, in many cases nascent policy concepts represent solutions in search of problems.[2] One ramification of this is a significant element of unpredictability in the development of policy proposals. There are some larger groups that are predictably interested in almost every proposal introduced in their sphere of interest. However, as new policy proposals develop, they can affect many groups with narrower interests that were not initially concerned with an issue. In fact, evolving policy proposals that transcend traditional boundaries may affect organizations that were previously inactive in that policy domain. These previously unaffected groups that are brought into the political debates of a policy domain new to them are known as "externality groups."[3] Salisbury argues that the "central importance of the newly prominent externality groups is that they further destabilize the policy-making process" by undermining the hegemony of peak associations.[4] There are important informational components to be considered as well.

The potential of externality groups to become involved in a policy debate magnifies the information challenge facing would-be coalition entrepreneurs. Whereas groups that have been active in a policy domain may develop reputations for consistently addressing certain issues in that domain, by definition this is not the case with externality groups entering that policy domain for the first time. Given the unpredictability of many policy proposals, especially those that find their window of opportunity through chance occurrences, it is often difficult to guess which externality groups may become involved in an issue domain.

This point is illustrated by Edward Laumann and David Knoke's example of a petroleum industry trade association's opposition to an announcement by the Federal Aviation Administration. The FAA announced that it intended to promulgate new regulations requiring detailed flight plans to be filed by pilots of noncommercial aircraft. To most observers there was little apparent connection between oil production and a requirement to file flight plans, but

> [the executive director of the petroleum-related trade association] realized that once detailed flight plans were on record with the FAA, the open-disclosure provisions of the Freedom of Information Act would allow anyone to learn where his member companies' planes were flying on their aerial explorations for oil, gas, and minerals. The alert director . . . saved the corporations potentially millions of dollars worth of secret data that might have fallen into the laps of their competitors.[5]

For aviation-related organizations, such as the Aircraft Owners and Pilots Association, with long-standing interests in regulations regarding flight plans, determining which organizations might come out of the woodwork on a given issue is not always a simple challenge.[6]

Certainly, policy proposals differ in their likelihood of attracting externality groups. Regular reauthorization bills for long-standing programs are less likely to attract outside interests than are new proposals designed to alter the status quo. Thus the information challenge would generally be less complicated for a group anticipating the reauthorization of funding for an existing highway project, for example, than it was for President Clinton's proposal to reorganize the health care system. However, in one case that took place in Kansas, even a simple ongoing highway project was susceptible to unpredicted attacks from environmentalists who discovered a rare frog and from Native Americans whose unmapped sacred grounds would have been disturbed. Indeed, environmental groups are often the classic example of an externality group.

To cope with information questions such as these, groups with broad scopes of interest develop larger monitoring capabilities where possible.[7] Organizations with extensive institutional links to other groups are advantaged in the collection of political intelligence.

Friend or Foe? Distinguishing Likely Allies from Opponents

In theory, the set of potential players on an issue can be divided into two subsets: potential allies and potential opponents. Early in an issue's life cycle, these divisions are neither fixed nor exclusive. Rather, they represent probabilistic calculations about the likely overlap in organizational interests and preferences. This leads to a problem of uncertainty. Organizations must determine the likely positions of other organizations before they begin the task of coalition building. As one lobbyist explained, "You've got to check with other people, because . . . you've got to know where your opposition is."

Given the information problems in the early stages of issue forma-tion, contacting groups that will eventually oppose your point of view gives them significant information that they might not have otherwise had. At a minimum, it can alert them that a policy change is afoot. It also conveys one's position, and it could convey extensive information about the political environment. As a strategic blunder, direct contact can provide the impetus for latent opposition to mobilize, expanding the scope of conflict.[8] As a tactical matter, it is clearly in a group's interest to let its opponents address the information problems on their own.

Edward Grefe suggests that coalition organizers trying to identify potential members should break down the traditional categories of allies and opponents into smaller subsets.[9] Specifically, likely allies can be conceived of as:

Family: These are employees, shareholders, retirees, spouses. . . .

Friends: Customers and suppliers, and others with an economic relation-ship to the company. . . .

Strangers: These are groups that might be interested in the issues if they know of the measure and understand its impact. Grefe includes in this category business organizations, academicians, the press, and communities in which the company has operations.[10]

Clearly a coalition broker has very different levels of information about the groups composing each of these categories. In the case of a corpora-tion, the policy stance of customers and suppliers will probably be better known (or at least more easily identified) than the views of the groups Grefe would label strangers, which would include externality groups. However, these "strangers" might be better known if there were institutional links between the organizations.

How do organizations overcome these information problems? For most groups, the experience and contacts of their government affairs staff is critical. Lobbyists who have worked in Washington and have observed the groups that are active in a policy domain develop a sense of what other groups value and the political and policy goals that they advocate. The opportunities for Washington representatives to meet one another and observe other groups in action are almost infinite. As regular participants in policy debates, Washington representatives see one another testify, read about one another's efforts in the *Washington Post* and *National Journal*, watch one another on the *News Hour*, meet one another at social and political events, and share sofas while waiting to see legislators and staffers. Yet many of these opportunities to observe representatives from other groups in action are somewhat random, and there are other, more systemic sources of information. Many lobbyists have connections that go beyond the expertise garnered as participant-observers. Most notably, some organizations are institutionally linked. We know from earlier studies that interest groups "talk" with one another. My interviews with interest group leaders collected data regarding the forums in which intergroup communication takes place, as well as group leader assessments of the relative importance of the different forums for political coordination. Additional research has been done on these issues by Laumann and Knoke as well as by John Heinz and his colleagues.[11] Laumann and Knoke examine information exchange between group dyads as a key to intergroup cooperation, differentiating between groups which share "regular and routine" information from those which share "candid and confidential" information. Heinz and his colleagues focus primarily on personal communications and acquaintance patterns of Washington group elites.

In the rest of this chapter I will focus on two general types of institutional links among organizations in the interest group universe and the role that these links play in addressing the information side of coordinating political action.

INTERGROUP LINKS

Some organizations are linked through the career paths of their staff members. This phenomenon has been described as a revolving door, in which staff members carry their experience and contacts between positions in the public and private sectors. Career moves facilitate the flow of information about organizational preferences, both through the flow of experiential capital and through increased direct communication. The second general form of intergroup link I will examine is what I call a "group interlock." Group interlocks are links that arise when an individual simultaneously works for more than one organization, whether it be on a board of directors, as a paid staff member, or as an outside legal counsel or representative.

These institutional links can provide effective conduits for the coordination of information exchange and group strategy, simplifying the intelligence-gathering efforts that would otherwise be required of organizations desiring to pursue collective strategies. If organizations are structurally or institutionally linked to one another, they do not face great challenges in "finding" one another (the first information problem of coordination), and there is a lower cost of discovering their preferences (the second information problem of coordination).

Though institutional links are not used on every issue, their very real presence also creates a loose but generally stable framework of relationships with policy sectors that can help provide form to the issue network models. In many cases, staff interlocks and coalitions are actually systemic factors of stability within fragmented policy spheres.

I will argue that groups who are able to overcome the information problem through interorganizational links have a distinct advantage over unrelated organizations, and these advantages enable them to develop collective action more effectively, though in some cases the institutional links may actually be sufficient to transcend the need for collective action. Because of this, I will argue that policy sectors with frequent linkages at the aggregate level are less likely to show long-term coalition activity. The paradox is that groups with institutional links have a greater *ability* to develop purposive political coalitions, but institutional links make it less *necessary* for them to join long-term coalitions. Conversely, groups with fewer institutional links have a more difficult time establishing coordination, but they may need it more.

Revolving Doors and Intergroup Coordination

Washington is well known for its fluid work environment. With approximately three thousand presidential appointments made after each quadrennial election cycle, Hugh Heclo has asked whether the United States is run by a "government of strangers."[12] Among executive branch appointees, Heclo notes,

> political interaction is less like regularly scheduled matches between competing teams of partisans (President versus Congress, Republicans versus Democrats) and more like a sandlot pick-up game, with a variety of strangers, strategies, and misunderstandings. Such working relationships as exist are created and recreated sporadically as the political players come and go. Each largely picks up his lore anew—how to make his way, look for support, and deal with officialdom. . . . Political executives have no common culture for dealing with the problems of governing, and it is seldom that they are around long enough or trust one another enough to acquire one.[13]

Staff turnover is high on Capitol Hill as well, and the story is not terribly different in the private and nonprofit sectors. Washingtonians generally do not spend their careers working for the same organization or firm. Washington is a mobile city.[14]

Much has been made of career paths among business, associations, and government that resemble revolving doors. In this paradigm, individuals cycle through industry-related positions, bringing the interests of major corporations into government when individuals enter government service and selling government influence to business when they leave public service. Writing in the late 1970s, Heclo describes the president's cabinet in these terms.

> The background of Carter's cabinet can be described in terms of movement among four great estates: academia, corporate business and law, the government bureaucracy, and (to a lesser extent) elective politics. . . . Obviously no one estate is able to dominate all of the top positions. Moreover, every cabinet secretary has seen service in more than one of the major sectors. While there is movement from lower to higher positions, few people move up through the ranks of a single organization or sector in order to reach the top slots. Rather they move in hierarchies that stretch across the estates. Lower academic or business positions are parlayed into higher political appointments; lower political appointments into higher business positions; and so on.[15]

The metaphor of a revolving door raises significant normative concerns about unethical influences in the policy-making process.[16] Concerned with issues of influence peddling and unfair advantage to government contractors who hire former government officials, Congress and the executive branch have moved to limit the access of former executive branch employees and high-level congressional staffers to decision makers for a period after the end of their government service. Executive branch officials face a lifetime ban on lobbying regarding "specific issues in which the former official participated 'personally and substantially.' "[17] Political scientists have tried to determine the degree to which revolving doors between the public and private sphere impact the policy-making process.[18] Salisbury and Paul Johnson have concluded that for most organizational representatives, substantive knowledge from government experience is deemed more important than personal contacts formed there.[19]

Political scientists are relatively familiar with movement patterns between government service and the private sector. Heclo has demonstrated that, contrary to the early impression that executive branch appointees repeatedly move back and forth between the public and private sectors, most executive branch appointees enter government and serve in the executive branch once, or at most twice, with their primary careers in the private sector.[20] However, little attention has been given to career movement within the organizational sector. Where Heclo and the Salisbury research team focused on the doors between interest groups and government, for the purposes of this chapter it is useful to think about the movement *among groups* and the effects of that movement upon intergroup communications and political action. Do the career paths of individuals moving among organizations enable or enhance political coordination and communication among those organizations?

In order to measure the impact of intergroup staff links, the key issues to be measured are the proportion of staff with experience in other organizations, the degree to which they serve as conduits of communication and political coordination, and the degree to which they function unidirectionally or bidirectionally.

If revolving doors between groups and government enable closer communications between actors in the public and private sectors, it is reasonable to hypothesize that doors between organizations are also an important link in the study of interest group coordination and cooperation. Though organizations hire some individuals from the Hill, most employees in the organizational sector come from other organizations. In fact, more organizations report hiring government affairs staffers with experience in other organizations than with experience in all branches of government combined (see table 5-1).

Table 5-1 shows that over 80 percent of the organizations active in the transportation, education, or civil rights sectors report having hired government affairs staff members with experience working in other organizations. In each policy domain, fewer groups boasted governmental affairs staff members with any kind of experience working for the federal government. Put another way, more organizations gain their experienced governmental affairs staff members from the ranks of persons who developed their expertise in other organizations than from those who worked for the government.

TABLE 5-1.
Percentage of Organizations Reporting Government Relations Staff Members with Previous Experience Working for the Federal Government or Other Organized Interests
(By Policy Sector)

	Prior Federal Government Experience (All Branches Combined)	Prior Organization/ Policy Experience	Sample N for Each Survey Item
Transportation	80.4	80.8	(46,47)
Education	70.8	82.9	(48,47)
Civil rights	72.4	83.3	(29,30)

For those individuals who do move from an agency or congressional staff position to an organization, this move is usually only the
first step on a long and complex journey that will take them through
a number of organizations before reaching their terminal positions.
What is more, at each step along the way, they contribute a wealth of
contacts, information, and experience to their new employer. The result
of this mobility and transfer of experience and contacts is a reduction
in the cost of information collection for the employer.

As a lobbyist for a national transportation corporation explained
that company's experience,

> I came from an organization that also had the same issues that I have
> here. We're almost sister [organizations]. It's not like I went from truck
> renting and leasing to the oil industries or something. That continues
> because we're still, we're all addressing the same issues. . . . I think that
> my company relies on me more to be the liaison with them [with the
> previous employer] than they did before, because they know I've been
> there, and I know the people, and I know the issues. . . . So I think that
> there's a reliance on me because of my background.

Intergroup moves are not limited to the early stages of an individual's career path but may continue at the top executive level. After
Richard Lesher announced his retirement as president of the U.S. Chamber of Commerce in 1997 after twenty-two years in that position, the
head of the American Trucking Association, Thomas J. Donohue, Jr.,
was tapped to fill the position.[21] Though there were clearly candidates
for the position within the Chamber of Commerce, such as the senior
vice president of the Chamber's membership policy group, the search
committee sought the experience and Washington contacts Donohue
could bring with him from the ATA. Prior to taking over the helm of
the ATA in 1984, Donohue served as a group vice president at the
Chamber from 1977 to 1984.[22]

In a true revolving door model of influence, we assume that individuals carry the experiences, interests, and contacts of former employers
with them when they move into a new position. If this is the case, we
would expect to see them, at the very least, functioning as conduits of
communication between current and former employers. Furthermore,
we would expect this communication to be bidirectional, with mutually
beneficial political coordination between current and former employers.
Conversely, in a purely atomistic political world, we would expect to
see former employees and former employers operating in a disjoint
manner, without political contacts particularly linked to employment
patterns. In fact, neither of these situations is the case.

A revolving door metaphor cannot be applied accurately to interest group professionals, because the portals of information, experience, and political connections flow in only one direction. Without question, individuals take their past experience and connections with them when they move to new positions. But they leave their loyalties behind, and former employers report almost unanimously that they initiate little contact with those who move on.

This is confirmed through two parallel question series on the survey instrument. First, respondents were asked to evaluate their staff members' connections to former employers. Second, they were asked about former staff members who had left the organization. These questions focused on whether the organizations were still in contact with those individuals, and whether those contacts were useful.

Among those 102 respondents who reported staff members with experience working for other associations, 50 percent of the combined sample stated that current staff contacts with former employers were "very useful," while only 14.3 percent of the respondents stated that such contacts were "not useful at all" (see table 5-2). Respondents from the transportation sample were more likely than respondents in the other fields to report useful staff contacts with former employers, though a difference in the population cannot be statistically inferred from this data alone.

A question regarding how important current staff members were specifically as "communications links" to their former employers turned up quite similar results (table 5-3). Approximately half of the groups noted that current staff members are "very important" communications links to their former employers, with respondents from the transportation domain again leading the pack.

TABLE 5-2.
Assessment of Usefulness to Organizations of Contacts between
Current Staff and their Former Employers
(By Percentage of Respondents)

	Very Useful	Fairly Useful	Not That Useful	Not Useful at All	N
Transportation	62.2	21.6	5.4	10.8	(37)
Education	42.1	18.4	18.4	21.1	(38)
Civil rights	43.5	34.8	13.0	8.7	(23)
Totals:	50.0	23.5	12.2	14.3	(98)

Note: χ^2 (6 d.f.) = 8.12782; prob. = 0.22889

TABLE 5-3.
Assessment of Importance to Organizations of Current Staff Members as
Communications Links to their Former Employers
(By Percentage of Respondents)

	Very Important	Important	Somewhat Important	Not Important at All	N
Transportation	59.0	12.8	12.8	15.4	(39)
Education	34.2	5.3	31.6	28.9	(38)
Civil rights	47.8	8.7	21.7	21.7	(23)
Totals:	47.0	9.0	22.0	22.0	(100)

Note: χ^2 (6 d.f.) = 8.42963; prob. = 0.20829
Some rows may not sum to 100 percent due to rounding.

These contacts with former employers are useful in part because they allow organizations to exchange information on positions. The chief executive from an association of mental health professionals noted the role of the group's close personal ties to a similar organization:

[W]e do work in coalition with them on a number of issues. It helps because the personal contact is already established. I know that if I need information, I know who I can call, and then I can count on that person to get me the information that I need. And it helps that the working relationship is already established. It just makes things a lot easier, rather than going into it cold with someone that I'm not sure what their agenda is across the table.

Beyond communication, a representative brings knowledge of past positions held by other groups, and enhances the ability of an organization to *anticipate* the position that representative's former employers will take on new issues. A representative from a professional association in the education domain gave this example:

[I]n fact, right before you came we were talking about a bill that a long time ago I had participated in when I was [representing] ACA in terms of helping to write it. And now, we're sort of on the other side of the fence here, but we know the people over there, and we know the intent behind the bill, so yeah, that's definitely helped.

Tables 5-2 and 5-3 show the connections between Washington representatives and their former employers only from the perspective of their current employer. However, when the same respondents were asked similar questions from the opposite perspective—former employers reporting their contacts with individuals who have moved on to other positions—there was a marked difference in the responses.

Former employees are generally considered neither important nor useful as contacts. When asked how important former staff members were in coordinating political action between the respondent's organization and the organization for whom former staff members currently worked, group leaders from all domains overwhelmingly reported that they were irrelevant (table 5-4). In fact, of 110 respondents, 71 (64.5 percent) could not think of a *single case* in which a former staff member was an important communications link to another organization.

These figures are strikingly different from the patterns reported in tables 5-2 and 5-3. While respondents tend to report useful contacts with former employers, they are not nearly as likely to report useful contacts with former colleagues who have left their current organization. Rather than a revolving door between groups, we see a door in which useful communication and political coordination flow predominantly in one direction. Individuals call on their former employers, but employers call upon former employees much less frequently.

In part this may be because individuals are likely to prefer their current positions to their former positions. If a staff member changed positions on his or her own initiative, we can infer preference. If the former position was terminated unilaterally by the former employer, we can assume that the staff member's loyalties may have waned due to the lack of reciprocal loyalty. The director of government affairs for an association active in children's issues pointed out the other side of the coin: "I think if you have a person that leaves under not optimal

---

TABLE 5-4.

Assessment of Importance of Relationships with Former Staff Members in Coordinating Political Action with Other Organizations (By Percentage of Respondents)

	Very Important	Important	Somewhat Important	Irrelevant	N
Transportation	10.8	13.5	16.2	59.5	(37)
Education	7.0	4.7	16.3	72.1	(43)
Civil rights	16.7	10.0	16.7	56.7	(30)
Totals:	10.9	9.1	16.4	63.6	(100)

Note: χ^2 (6 d.f.) = 4.09319; prob. = 0.66407
Some rows may not sum to 100 percent due to rounding.

circumstances, you know, leaves at a bad time, you know, you feel like they've deserted you, you have some negative feelings, sure, I think you're gonna have a lot of that."

There is an important information asymmetry behind this finding. A former employee knows what his or her former employer is (1) likely to be interested in and (2) likely to by working on. There is, however, no such automatic information advantage for the former employer, who has no way of knowing what the former employee's new job entails, what the former staffer's new employer is interested in, or what the former staffer's new employer is likely to be working on, *unless the former staffer reports this information.* Organizations may have a contact in their former employees, but they do not have an automatic source of knowledge about another organization.

Consider the hypothetical but typical case of Harold and Anne, government relations representatives for two organizations. Harold used to work for Anne's organization, but has since moved on to his current position in a recently formed group down the street. When confronted with a new legislative proposal, Harold and Anne (both inclined toward collective action strategies, for reasons that were discussed in chapter 3) face two information dilemmas. First, they must ascertain which other organizations might be interested in the new issue. Second, they must find out which of the interested organizations are likely to hold similar positions on the issue. They wish to answer both of these questions without unnecessarily stirring up the potential opposition and needlessly expanding the scope of conflict.

Harold's information advantage comes into play. Having worked for Anne's organization, he has a working knowledge of the positions that group has held in the past, its decision-making processes, and the positions it is likely to hold in the future. As a former employee, he has a substantial corpus of confidential and internal information that is significantly deeper than that which "everyone" knows from the reputation of Anne's group. Harold, in practice, has a high probability of knowing whether or not he should contact Anne about the issue. Harold is empowered to coordinate political action with Anne if he thinks it appropriate. Anne, on the other hand, has significantly less basis on which to judge Harold's likely positions. Though Anne may know Harold well as an individual, her knowledge of Harold's organization is significantly shallower by definition, limited to past observations and reputation. Moreover, the fact that Harold's group was recently formed increases the level of uncertainty.

For these reasons, staff career paths can be an important source of information for organizations trying to answer the information questions inherent in political coordination. The larger an organization is, the more staff links exist, and the greater its information advantage is likely to be. The caveat is that information flows through the revolving door in only one direction; the information advantages travel with a staff member from position to position.

Intergroup Coordination via Board and Staff Interlocks

Communications between staff members and former employers are certainly not the only institutional links that can be used to overcome the information challenges inherent in coordinating the political activities of organizations. A second general forum is found in the group interlock.

Students of sociology, business management, and public administration have long documented the phenomenon of interlocking corporate directorates. When an individual serves on the board of directors of two or more companies, those boards are said to be interlocked.[23] Researchers have studied interlocking corporate directorates in an effort to understand the degree to which cooperation and coordination within the business community are due to institutional, economic, class, and general ideological factors.[24]

This concept has rarely been applied to the study of interest groups, but it is a helpful construct for examining the degree of atomization and interaction among groups. However, there is no reason to restrict the use of the interlock construct to the board level. I examine group interlocks at several organizational levels. A group interlock is a link between organizations in which at least one individual simultaneously holds a formal position of responsibility in two or more organizations. This definition subsumes the traditional definition of the corporate interlocking directorates but goes beyond the immediate board of directors to include staff members working concurrently for two organizations, as well as lobbyists, attorneys, and other individuals who represent the interests of two or more organizations in public and private forums.

Though a good deal of research on interlocking directorates has been based on theories of conspiracies or of a power elite, the concept need not be linked to such wide-reaching theories of class structure.[25] For my purposes, it is an open and instructive hypothesis to be explored.

Interlocks, to the degree that they exist, could be useful in explaining one mechanism for communication and coordination of political action between organizations. The study of interlocking directorates traditionally examines interlocks as the dependent variable (e.g., as the result of class integration), or as evidence of class cohesion. Here I examine interlocks at the board and staff level as an independent variable that may or may not enable intergroup communication and coordination, rather than as evidence that such communication and coordination take place.

Board members are actively involved in both setting and reviewing the policy positions of the organizations they oversee. Similarly, hired outside lobbyists, Washington attorneys, and other outside group representatives are active participants in the organizational policy process. Because of the specialization and expertise valued in outside representatives, they may well represent other organizations with related interests, making them an attractive potential bridge for information exchange. How prevalent are group interlocks, and to what degree are they used to overcome the information challenges facing organizations that pursue political coordination?

Board Interlocks

Almost all organizations active in Washington have a board of directors. All but 3 of 129 organizations responding to an inquiry about a board of directors affirmed that they did have some form of board. These ranged in size from 4 to 200 members. The mean board size was 31.7 members.

Most of these boards have at least one board interlock with other organizations. Eighty-nine groups (approximately 71 percent of the respondents) stated that their board had members who simultaneously served on other boards of directors. Thirteen groups reported that they did not have any interlocks, and twenty-four respondents (one-fifth) did not know whether any individuals served on other boards.[26]

As table 5-5 shows, group representatives active in the transportation field were significantly more likely to know of interlocks than representatives active in either education or civil rights.

But how significant are these interlocks? Do staffers effectively utilize board interlocks to overcome the information problem? Can staffers gain information about the positions, preferences, and activities of other organizations by virtue of board interlocks?

TABLE 5-5.
Percentage of Respondents Identifying an Interlock between their Board of Directors and other Organizations

	Interlock	No Interlock	Do Not Know	N
Transportation	87.0	6.5	6.5	(46)
Education	61.2	14.3	24.5	(49)
Civil rights	61.3	9.7	29.0	(31)

Note: $N = 126$, χ^2 (4 d.f.) = 10.3084; prob. = 0.03554

In order for a specific interlock to be useful to the government affairs staff, it is necessary at the very least for the staff members to be aware of it. Of those representatives who know that there are interlocks on their board of directors, 88 percent (59 percent of the total sample) could identify at least one interlocking director by name and at least one of the organizations on the board of which he or she serves. More significantly, these government affairs staffers reported that the interlocks were beneficial to their work. Respondents were asked whether there were specific advantages for their organization available by virtue of having interlocking board members. The vast majority of groups answered in the affirmative, with many groups labeling interlocks "very beneficial"(see table 5-6). Group leaders offered a wide range of examples to describe the benefits their organizations receive through group interlocks. The most frequently cited answer was "information about what other organizations are doing," or, as the head lobbyist for one educational organization put it, "reconnaissance shared back and forth about what one group or another is doing."

This intelligence sharing between board members can be an important source of information as governmental affairs staff members address the first two questions of political coordination, ascertaining what organizations are likely to be interested in an issue and what their likely positions are. One trucking representative explained:

> I can speak to that because many of [our board members] are active, obviously chairmen or CEOs of their own companies, or past chairmen, so we have found some synergy there by knowing that a particular CEO's own company is doing something in an area, then he can offer that we would work with his Washington office, or he could at least share information as to what their company's policy is or strategy is.

TABLE 5-6.
Assessment of Benefits for Respondent's Organization of
Interlocking Board Members
(By Percentage of Respondents)

	Very Beneficial	Somewhat Beneficial	No Advantages	N
Transportation	56.1	29.2	14.6	(41)
Education	28.6	46.4	25.0	(28)
Civil rights	42.9	50.0	7.1	(14)

Note: N = 83, χ^2 (4 d.f.) = 6.68612; prob. = 0.15343
Some rows may not sum to 100 percent due to rounding.

Government affairs staff members tend to have limited direct contact with board members. For active interlocks, however, that point is insignificant, as they have extensive contact with the top level of the organizational hierarchy. In most organizations, the president or executive director serves as the key point of access to the board of directors. Thus, a government affairs representative from a highway lobby described the path of intelligence from board members this way: "[T]ypically that's something that will come across my president's desk and wind up on my desk—some things that we should be interested in . . . you know, just FYI sort of things. But that is the trend, so we end up with a lot of strange cross combinations that way."

A trucking firm noted a similar theme:

[Do you think board members serve as conduits of political information?] With respect to the political community, yes, I think so. Maybe not with competitive issues, but I think that . . . particularly this is fostered by the Business Roundtable, which, you know, is a CEO organization. They're looking for as much help as they can get on their own issues, so they like to bring up, you know, "we need to work on this," or "we need [your company's] help." So I think that they do, the ones that are politically attuned.

We get some good ideas from [board interlocks]. We get some good ideas sometimes, and it makes some interesting and useful connections.

Organizations capitalize on these board interlocks in several ways, and in some cases, the interlocks are themselves institutionalized. In the field of higher education, one respondent reported that "the American Council of Education has one or two seats that they call 'association seats,' and every so many years we are eligible to have our member sit on their board, I believe it's for a year, because our association comes up in the rotation. But that is really a function of our organization." This pattern also holds true in vocational education, where one organizational representative described the composition of her board of directors as "members of the organization, eleven regional representatives, four officers. I'm an ex officio member. The American Vocational Association always wants a liaison person on our board."

Board interlocks are useful not only to gather information but to convey information to other groups. A trade association official explained:

When you are trying a coalition bill on an issue that is very important to you as an organization, you can sit down with your committee members or board members and say, "We can sure use some help from other organizations. We need your help in helping them move and pick up their priorities and adopting this particular position, getting them to at least play a minor role. So, as the board member of the Food Processors (or the Grocery Manufacturers or the Milk Producers or the Chamber of Commerce, or whatever), would you put in a good word there?"

Or, [suppose] those guys have taken a contrary position; you do what you can to neutralize them, because they are hurting you and your point of view. So that kind of cross-fertilization occurs [through board members].

Representatives of groups active in transportation policy were not only most likely to know of board interlocks but most likely to identify interlocks as "very beneficial." This pattern was even more striking when respondents were asked specifically whether "members of the board serve as a path of communication and/or information to and from other organizations on whose boards they serve" (see table 5-7). Overall, approximately 76 percent of the groups with board interlocks affirmed that this type of interlock was used for communications and the exchange of information. The three samples differed significantly, though, and 84 percent of the groups in the transportation sample with interlocks answered yes, while only 67 percent of the civil rights sample did so.

Again, we see that the pattern of information links—one route to overcoming the information problem in political coordination—is not randomly distributed across issue domains. Transportation groups are not only better linked through staff connections but better integrated at the board level, and they report board interlocks to be more useful sources of information than organizations active in education or civil rights do.

Third-Party Interlocks
The last type of interlock is a third-party interlock. Third-party interlocks are those individuals who represent two or more organiza-

TABLE 5-7.
Percentage of Respondents Identifying Members of Their Board as a
Path of Communication to and from Other Organizations on
Whose Boards They Serve

	Yes	No	Do Not Know	N
Transportation	84.2	5.3	10.5	(38)
Education	71.4	25.0	3.6	(28)
Civil rights	66.7	11.1	22.2	(18)
Total:	76.2	13.1	10.7	(84)

Note: χ^2 (4 d.f.) = 9.04231; prob. = 0.06005

tions on a retainer or contract basis, though they are neither internal employees nor board members of those organizations. The most common examples are outside attorneys, lobbyists, and consultants. Whether thought of as "outside counsel" or "hired guns," most of these individuals work on behalf of several organizations at the same time.

When individuals with multiple employers are considered, the most frequently discussed questions generally deal with the ethical issue of conflicting interests; for example, can attorneys or representatives work for several organizations without compromising the interests or proprietary information of any of these groups? However, when considering the coordination of political action, we need to examine this issue from the opposite perspective: Do organizations that employ the same outside counsel or lobbyist benefit from this third-party interlock? Does their mutual representative enable the development of interaction, communication, and collective action between them? Do these organizations choose to share information through that third-party interlock?

In a political universe best characterized as atomistic, we would expect that third-party interlocks would not be particularly important organizational links. We would further expect that organizations with this type of interlock would not use these interlocks to coordinate political action on a regular basis. On the other hand, to the degree that these interlocks exist, are recognized, and are used to share information between organizations, the universe in which they operate can less accurately be depicted as atomistic. In the latter case, these interlocks are likely to simplify and encourage the coordination of political action by providing a crucial source of political information.

Two examples of third-party interlocks are outside attorneys and outside lobbyists. Approximately four out of five groups in the primary samples employed outside legal counsel. This proportion was approximately equal for the transportation and education samples, both of which hovered around 80 percent. Approximately half of the civil rights sample reported hiring an outside legal counsel. However, organizations hire outside lobbyists and representatives much less frequently than they hire outside attorneys and legal counsel (see table 5-8). Only one individual interviewed did not know whether his organization employed outside counsel.

Of the organizations with outside attorneys, a sizable number reported that their counsel represented other organizations active in the policy domain related to their sample (i.e., transportation, education, or civil rights). As table 5-9 shows, the rates for groups that are active primarily within the sample domain are quite different from those for outsiders (also known as "externality groups") that are active within the domain only on occasion. Groups that were primarily active in the

TABLE 5-8.

Percentage of Organizations Employing Outside Attorneys and Lobbyists

	Attorney			Lobbyist			
	Yes	No	Do Not Know	Yes	No	Do Not Know	N
Transportation	83.0	14.9	2.1	51.1	48.9	0.0	(47)
Education	80.0	20.0	0.0	18.0	82.0	0.0	(50)
Civil rights	50.0	50.0	0.0	23.3	73.3	3.3	(30)

Note: Some rows may not sum to 100 percent due to rounding.

sample domain are significantly more likely to have attorneys that represented other clients in that field than externality groups are.[27]

The situation is quite different in the case of outside lobbyists, where externality groups are just as likely to have lobbyist interlocks within the sample domain as domain groups are (see table 5-10).

Many organizations hire attorneys, and it seems that they hire from within their own domain. It is also clear that domain groups are much more likely than externality groups to have an outside attorney who represents other organizations in the sample domain. Attorney interlocks are therefore most likely to reinforce the relationships among domain players and tend to be intradomain links. Outside lobbyists are hired much less frequently than outside attorneys, and they are

TABLE 5-9.

Percentage of Organizations Whose Outside Attorneys Represent Other Organizations in the Sample Domain

	Yes	No	Do Not Know	N
Transportation sample	69.2	10.3	20.5	(39)
Transportation groups	83.3	5.6	11.1	(18)
Other groups	57.1	14.3	28.6	(21)
Education sample	37.5	7.5	55.0	(40)
Education groups	54.5	4.5	40.9	(22)
Other groups	16.7	11.1	72.2	(18)
Civil rights sample	57.1	21.4	21.4	(14)
Civil rights groups	100.0	0.0	0.0	(4)
Other groups	40.0	30.0	30.0	(10)

Note: Some rows may not sum to 100 due to rounding.

TABLE 5-10.
Percentage of Organizations Whose Outside Lobbyists Represent Other
Organizations in the Sample Domain

	Yes	No	Do Not Know	N
Transportation sample	70.8	16.7	12.5	(24)
Transportation groups	70.0	20.0	10.0	(10)
Other groups	71.4	14.3	14.3	(14)
Education sample	77.8	0.0	22.2	(9)
Education groups	80.0	0.0	20.0	(5)
Other groups	75.0	0.0	25.0	(4)
Civil rights sample	14.3	57.1	28.6	(7)
Civil rights groups[a]	0.0	0.0	0.0	(0)
Other groups	14.3	57.1	28.6	(7)

[a] No group in the sample identifying itself as a "civil rights group" per se reported
hiring outside representatives or lobbyists at all. From their point of view, lobbying
expertise lay within the organization itself.

not significantly more likely to be hired by domain organizations than
externality groups active within the same domain. This in itself would
imply more home-court preference when hiring attorneys than when
selecting lobbyists. Hence, attorney interlocks are more likely to be
linked with enabling long-term, intradomain coalitions, and lobbyists
can enable both intradomain and short-term, interdomain coalitions.

These findings open up several hypotheses for future research. It
may be that attorneys and lobbyists both specialize to a similar degree,
but groups hire outside attorneys from their home domain while they
hire outside lobbyists from the relevant issue domain as needs warrant.
Alternately, these findings could be explained by specialization among
attorneys and generalization among lobbyists. Whereas groups hire
their home-court attorneys, they use a lobbyist over time without consideration of the issue field. If this were the case, however, the percentages in table 5-10 should be proportional between domains to the
percentage of groups in each domain, not just similar between domain
groups and externality groups.

In order for third-party interlocks to function as mechanisms for
information exchange, "linked" organizations need to know who the
attorney or lobbyist's other clients are. This is in fact much more common than might be expected, primarily because organizations are quite
cautious about entering into situations where conflicts of interest might

TABLE 5-11.
Percentage of Respondents Who Could Name Other Organizations
Represented by Their Outside Counsel

	Yes	No	N
Transportation	89.3	10.7	(28)
Education	75.0	25.0	(16)
Civil rights	75.0	25.0	(8)

arise. Such information actually lays the foundation for potential cooperation.

In cases where outside attorneys represent other organizations in
the sample domain, the vast majority of group leaders can identify
other clients (see table 5-11). As table 5-12 shows, the pattern is similar
for organizations with outside lobbyists or representatives.

TABLE 5-12.
Percentage of Respondents Who Could Name Other Organizations
Represented by Their Outside Lobbyists

	Yes	No	N
Transportation	83.3	16.7	(18)
Education	75.0	25.0	(8)
Civil rights	100.0	0.0	(1)

PUTTING IT TOGETHER

The bulk of this chapter has shown that there are significant institutional
links between organizations at the board and staff levels and that many
of these links can and do serve as sources of information for government
affairs representatives. This information is a critical component of political coordination between organized interests.

Organizations that have institutionalized mechanisms for gathering this information have an advantage in coordinating action with
other organizations, in part because they can identify potential partners
and adversaries more efficiently. Moreover, these institutional links
between organizations can serve as nodes for action as well as information collection.

If the general hypothesized connection between institutional links
and political coordination is correct, we would expect organizations

with more institutional links to have less difficulty forming purposive coalitions. As observed in chapter 3, some organizations join established coalitions in order to gain information. On the other hand, organizations with institutional links have less need to rely on long-term coalitions as sources of information. We would thus expect to see a positive relationship between links and active, politically oriented coalitions, and a negative relationship between links and membership in long-term, information-related coalitions. Similarly, we would expect issue domains with more links to have more capacity to form purposive coalitions, but less reliance upon coalitions for information purposes.

In examining intergroup links, we see a clear trend. Of the three issue domains examined, organizations active in the transportation sector exhibit significantly more links to other organizations across the board than do organizations active in either education policy or civil rights.

Much of the data presented so far in this chapter are summarized in table 5-13, and a striking pattern emerges. The transportation domain has the greatest number of institutional links and reports the highest usefulness of those links in almost every category. Conversely,

TABLE 5-13.
Summary of Institutional Links
(By Percentage of Respondents)

	Transportation	Education	Civil Rights
Current employee			
Very useful contacts	62	42	44
Very important link	59	34	47
Current employee			
At least somewhat important link	84.6	71.1	78.3
Irrelevant	15.4	28.9	21.7
Former employees			
At least somewhat important link	40.5	28.7	43.4
Irrelevant	59.5	72.1	56.7
Board interlocks present	87	61.2	61.3
Board interlocks very beneficial	56	28.6	42
Board interlock serves as information source	84.2	71.4	66.2
Organization shares lawyer	69	37.5	57.1
Organization shares lobbyist	70.8	77.8	14.3

organizations in the education sample consistently report the lowest level of linkage and the least benefit from those linkages. Though the differences are not always large, the sheer consistency of the pattern is remarkable.

Why does the transportation domain almost invariably appear at the top of the list of linkages? Conversely, what (or who) is missing from the education domain that leaves the domain with consistently fewer interorganizational links? In large part, transportation stands out because the majority of the Washington representatives active in the domain represent business interests in the form of corporations and trade associations. Few corporations are headquartered in Washington, though many have a branch office there to coordinate their federal relations. However, outsourcing personnel requirements—in this case, hiring outside legal counsel and lobbyists—is a long-standing part of corporate culture. Corporations are also in a better position financially to bring in hired guns and keep them on retainer than are many of the smaller organizations active in the civil rights or education domain. Corporate board members generally serve on several boards, and that is also reflected in this data.

As noted in chapter 2, however, the education domain sees comparatively little action by business-related organizations. The majority of organizational actors in this domain are associations representing educators, administrators, and educational institutions. The civil rights domain occupies a middle ground. Though there are a significant number of business-related trade associations active in this contentious domain, individual corporations often try to avoid participating in the civil rights debates directly where doing so might have lasting side effects. In an era of boycotts, corporate representatives note that it is generally safer to rely on a trade association to speak for the industry than to take a chance on being perceived as opposing civil rights. Indeed, corporate officers testifying before Congress often appear officially on behalf of the trade association and make comments regarding the effects of civil rights legislation upon their own companies with great delicacy.

The most important result of this disproportionately high number of interorganizational links in the transportation domain is that the well-linked organizations do not need to focus as much attention on developing lasting coalition relationships with other groups.

Organizations which are linked to other groups through internal links (staff members who come on board from previous jobs with their Rolodexes intact, or board or staff interlocks) have built-in conduits to other groups for information exchange, communication, and coordination of political activities. Organizations without these institutional links are more likely to seek out external relationships, such as standing coalition structures, to mimic the advantages of internal contacts. Thus, the link-rich transportation domain exhibits the highest level of short-term coalition activity and lowest level of long-term coalition activity (see table 5-14). Many organizations in the transportation domain simply do not need to join long-term coalitions to pursue their goals with other organizations.

Institutional links are *enabling* factors. Their presence does not guarantee that information will in fact be transferred any more than the presence of a door guarantees that someone will walk through it. Thus, attempts to measure their impact upon coalition formation across the board must be made with the caveat of close interpretation: the effect of intergroup links on information transfer will be large for some groups on some issues, but not for all groups, and certainly not for any groups on every issue. This probabilistic effect can be measured using regression analysis.

In this regression, I measure the systemic impact of each type of link discussed in this chapter upon the *overall* ease with which groups report forming short-term coalitions on all issues. The regression takes the form:

$$E(\text{ease of formation}) = \beta_0 + \beta_1 \text{link1} + \beta_2 \text{link2} + \beta_3 \text{link3} + \beta_4 \text{link4} + \beta_5 \text{link5} + \varepsilon$$

and

$$
\begin{aligned}
E(\text{ease of formation}) = \beta_0 &+ \beta_1 \text{interlock identification} \\
&+ \beta_2 \text{current staff link} \\
&+ \beta_3 \text{past staff link} + \beta_4 \text{outside lawyer} \\
&+ \beta_5 \text{outside lobbyist} + \varepsilon
\end{aligned}
$$

The dependent variable, ease of short-term coalition formation, is a response on a five-point scale to the statement "Short-term coalitions

TABLE 5-14.
Percentage of Organizations Reporting Different Coalition Strategies as "Very Important" or "Important"

	One-Time	Recurrent	Long-Term
Transportation	77.8	65.2	56.5
Education	54.0	72.0	70.0
Civil rights	61.3	83.9	80.6

are easy to form." Responses ranged from 1 (strongly agree) to 5 (strongly disagree). The independent variables are the ability to identify board interlocks (a dummy variable coded 1 if respondents could identify specific interlocks), the importance ascribed to current staff members as communications links to their former employers, the importance ascribed to past staff members as communications links to their current employers, and two other links represented in this regression with a dummy variable: the use of an outside attorney or outside lobbyist by the organization. The results are reported in table 5-15.

With the exception of links through past staff members, all coefficients show the expected sign; that is, they are consistent with the hypothesis that links enable coalition formation. Furthermore, "current staff link" achieves statistical significance as an explanatory variable at the .05 level. That other independent variables are not statistically significant is not surprising, given the fact that these are *enabling* rather than deterministic variables.

In the theoretical argument I have been presenting, I have taken an institutional perspective, in effect turning Frank Lloyd Wright's famous dictum of architecture, "form follows function," on its head. The relationships presented in table 5-15 do not represent a case of endogeneity. Groups very rarely establish links of this kind *in order* to build (or in anticipation of building) short-term coalitions. Rather,

TABLE 5-15.
Ordinary Least Squares Estimate of Link Impact on Ease in
Coalition Formation[a]

Independent Variable	Estimated Coefficient	Standard Error	T-Statistic
Intercept	2.40102	0.25761	9.32039
ID board interlock	−0.22364	0.18855	−1.18612
Current staff link importance	−0.15438	0.07099	−2.17454
Past staff link importance	0.02587	0.22184	0.28789
Lawyer	−0.14131	0.22184	−0.63698
Lobbyist	−0.05394	0.19699	−0.27385

Note: R-squared was approximately .08, but this is not relevant since the model measures the effects of specific independent variables but does not try to explain the entire dependent variable. Clearly, a full prediction of whether groups were likely to coalesce with each other would require consideration of whether they agreed on policy issues.
Number of Observations: 84

function follows form. Given the presence of staff members, lobbyists, attorneys, and board members with connections to other organizations, group leaders looking for information follow the wisdom of George Plunkitt's famous dictum: "I seen my opportunities and I took 'em."[28]

CONCLUSION

To reiterate the theme developed at the beginning of this chapter, collecting information about potential allies and adversaries is a necessary first stage of coordinating political activities. Intergroup links provide one avenue for organizations to gather that information when the links are relevant to the issue at hand. Not all links provide the same level of information, though. Links to former employers are reported to be much more helpful than links to former employees. Though group interlocks provide useful data on many occasions, these information sources in and of themselves do not "cause" coalitions to form. Coalitions gel with the exchange of benefits brokered by the founding core members of a nascent coalition.

There is clear evidence that links do enable some organizations to gather information with relative ease, and there is evidence that these domains exhibiting high degrees of institutional links also exhibit a high use of purposive coalitions relative to other domains that make more extensive use of long-term and information-based coalitions. However, linkages are only a part of the story in explaining political coordination and coalition behavior. Of the linkages examined, only "links through current staff members" is a statistically significant independent variable in explaining ease of coalition formation. To pursue a deeper understanding of the mechanisms for information exchange in coalition formation and to introduce the concept of grassroots partners in a Washington-based coalition, we turn in the next chapter to a case study of the Generalized System of Preferences Coalition and the advantages that changes in technology bring to coalition brokers.

6

Communication and Technological Developments in Political Coalitions

INTRODUCTION

The flow of information is crucial in all stages of coalition building. As noted in the previous chapter, institutional links can help coalition brokers estimate the interest and preferences of potential coalition members. These links can also simplify the initial contacts between groups in a coalition. Institutional links, however, are certainly not the only means by which coalition brokers communicate with other interests, and with the development of better communications technologies, the work of coalition brokers is getting easier. In this chapter, I will discuss the manner in which technological developments are simplifying the efforts of coalition brokers inside the Washington Beltway to expand their coalitions to the grassroots.

Computer technology has finally come of age. A majority of Americans now use computers in their daily lives. With this transformation of high-tech into standard operating procedures, the face of political coalitions is changing. Technology is bringing the world of grassroots coalition formation into real time.

TECHNOLOGY AND THE GRASSROOTS: THE CASE OF THE GSP COALITION

It is worthwhile for illustrative purposes to present a case that seems to exemplify my model of coalitions while simultaneously pointing out a developing trend that will dramatically enhance the ability of potential coalition members to find and recruit one another over the next few years. The case itself takes place in the early 1990s, and it indicates a significant increase in the role of technology in coalition building that has only accelerated since then. The case is offered not in an attempt to prove or argue a thesis, but rather to illustrate.

Scholars, like the journalistic pundits and commentators of our time, have frequently noted the role that changing technologies play in our political lives.[1] As Ithiel de Sola Pool noted in 1983, "Electronic media . . . allow for more knowledge, easier access, and freer speech than were ever enjoyed before."[2] Technological developments have not escaped the attention of organizational representatives, who have been quick to pick up cutting-edge tools that might provide an organizational advantage for their causes. The use of computers by organized interests dates back at least to the 1960s, when Richard Viguerie turned to computerized databases to usher in the now familiar direct mail techniques for fundraising.[3]

By the early 1990s most Washington-based coalitions had replaced their mailing lists with fax lists as the standard mode of communication and updates between meetings.[4] Though the fax itself has become commonplace throughout American society, Washington organizations have followed the technology curve more closely than the average American. As fax modems have become standard equipment on personal computers and software compatibility has increased, hand-fed fax machines are losing ground among Washington organizations for regularized communication. Indeed, "action alerts" and coalition updates are now frequently written, compiled, and mass-faxed to coalition members from a telephone database without any need for the coalition leader to print a hard copy. The impact of this is relatively straightforward: the communications choke hold on mobilization is being reduced as the time required for mass communication approaches zero.

The Generalized System of Preferences

The case below revolves around the reaction of importers and retailers to the expected expiration of the Generalized System of Preferences (GSP). GSP is a tariff program that allows the duty-free entry of imports from certain less developed countries. It is part of a nexus of programs based on the principle of "trade, not aid." In its simplest form, GSP is intended to provide an open American market in which developing countries can sell their products. A core member of the GSP coalition explained: "The idea is that you provide a market for a country like Bangladesh to sell watches, and that will be better for Bangladesh than sending them aid. And that's true. It's a tariff concession program that's sanctioned by the General Agreement on—GATT—Tariffs and Trade." In addition to the pure economic benefits that foster development rather than dependence, the GSP has provisions that allow its use to work on human rights issues and intellectual property issues.

A domestic side effect is that American companies and corporations that import merchandise under GSP provisions get duty-free treatment.

For some products, like toys, the difference in the price is significant: 12 percent duties are untied for use elsewhere.

The GSP Coalition was brokered in response to a concrete event. On 4 July 1993, the GSP program was scheduled to expire. As coalition members related the story,

> because of the transition, the Clinton Administration was very slow to realize they had a problem with GSP. They figured it out by February [1993] that they had to do something to get GSP extended. They also realized that GSP was a wonderful opportunity to give something to Russia that wasn't going to cost very much. Bypass Most Favored Nation tariffs and go directly duty free. So, they wrote up a little bill that extended GSP for a short period of time and provided the benefits to Russia.
>
> So, we were all on the side of the Administration, [and that] helps, but we were concerned because this was a little trade bill, and it had a revenue impact because there were lost revenues once the revenues were cranked into the baseline. So if you want to continue to not collect these revenues—never mind that we haven't collected them for twenty years—there was a budget impact. It was $800 million dollars give or take. And the problem was that we couldn't move it as a straight trade bill because they couldn't figure out how to pay for it. So we had to go on budget.

The GSP coalition is a particularly interesting example to explore for two reasons. First, the coalition demonstrates the efficiency and efficacy of grassroots communication in an era of fiscal constraints.

> This [the Omnibus Budget and Reconciliation Act] was a 500 billion-dollar tax and budget package. Our program was 791 million dollars. It was a microscopic flea, you know, a gnat on the backside of a ten-ton gorilla and that's the way the administration lobbyists on this characterized it. I mean the amount of money we were talking about was nothing more than a rounding error and yet we generated thousands, thousands of letters.

Second, the GSP coalition came only five years after a similar trade coalition effort with many of the same players, who were able to compare the changing role of technology in the coalition-building effort.

The Lobbying Environment for GSP

The international trade community, according to groups that participate in it, is relatively small: "People here in town who actually work on this stuff—it's almost like a family, it's so small. And so you see the same people over and over again." Related to the international trade community, numerous coalitions have arisen, such as the USA NAFTA

Coalition, the China Coalition, the GSP Coalition, and the Joint Industry Coalition (on Customs). These coalitions, while independent, have significant membership overlap due to the interrelatedness of their issues.

> You see the same people over and over again. Slightly different groups of characters in each one of these meetings. For instances, there's some people who only do customs and won't show up at someplace else. But some of the people who do customs are really interested in GSP because there's a whole customs issue that is involved with GSP. . . . It's just the same group, different meeting.

While the rise of externality groups in politics increases the likelihood that there will be new and unexpected players in lobbying coalitions, recurrent relationships among domain groups and externality groups are cropping up with increasing frequency. The director of government relations for a group of retailers described the increasing connections between two of her responsibilities:

> In some cases, you do get some cross-fertilization. I mean, I do environmental issues and trade issues, which happens to be so hot—[i.e.,] the sort of nexus between environment and trade. I'm starting to find my environment people showing up at trade meetings and vice versa. And its really confusing. Because it used to be for a long time there would be environmental people over here and trade people over here. "Never the twain shall meet." But it's getting all confused now.

With the increasing overlap of organizational interests, group representatives develop recurrent working relationships with externality organizations, knowing that their "strange-bedfellow" relationship might not be a one-time occurrence.

Formation of the Coalition

The impending expiration of the Generalized System of Preferences was a direct economic threat to importers. As of 5 July 1993, importers would have to pay significant tariffs on goods that they had been importing duty-free. The net effect on the federal budget of GSP's expiration would be $791 million in additional annual revenue. Representatives from the affected trade associations believed that under the political pressures for deficit reduction, an independent trade bill to extend the GSP would be an impossible sell. Congress seemed unlikely to reject an automatic infusion of almost $800 million in new revenue. An alternative to seeking an independent trade bill on the obscure issue was to lobby the House Ways and Means Committee to insert a provision extending GSP into the 1993 Omnibus Budget and Reconciliation Act, where its fate would be tied to the approval or rejection of the overall budget package.

As one would expect, the nascent GSP Coalition began with a handful of founding (core) members, each of which had a substantial economic interest in the GSP. According to one founding member, "We organized it here in town with some issue leaders. You know, from various trade associations and lawyers and the usual." As underdogs in a hostile environment, the core members deliberately chose to expand the scope of conflict. The core members moved to expand their coalition by contacting local businesses and corporations throughout the United States. Core members agreed that building a grassroots coalition with broad constituency voices was the best strategy to protect the GSP provisions.

> It wasn't that anybody [in Congress] hated GSP or anybody had any problem with GSP. It was just that, is it worth the $800 million dollars? And what the hell is GSP anyway? And why should I care? And so *our* job was to make sure that this was on everybody's radar screen and that we weren't simply relying on the administration to sell it for us because the administration had a lot of other water to carry in this budget reconciliation package. So we decided that . . . the way to win this issue was not for me to go visit with all these people [on the Hill] and tell them how important GSP was—that wasn't going to get it on anybody's radar screen. The trade people knew about it but nobody else did. The way to win this issue was to hear from people back home about how important this program really was.

Expanding the scope of conflict required notifying a broadly distributed set of importers and related business concerns. The core members focused on exploiting established links among customs brokers, trade attorneys, and their clients. With each customs broker representing potentially hundreds of clients, regular newsletters to those clients provided a ready-made forum for the coalition to make itself known to potential members. Brokers and trade attorneys placed notices in their newsletters informing clients that GSP would expire soon and instructing concerned firms to contact one of the core members. The results were described by a core member in charge of responding to information requests:

> I was getting an average of six, seven, eight phone calls a day from people out there [saying], "What do I do?" It got so bad that I couldn't keep up with the phone calls and I had the receptionist just saying, "Just give us your fax number." Some of these people in this coalition I never talked

to. I just faxed them out a message. They would call in, give me their fax number, they got an immediate message with instructions on how to write, cost them nothing. Most effective thing I ever did in my life.

The message faxed to potential coalition members focused directly upon the economic threat to the recipients, mixed with a dash of hyperbole.

We got the word out that everybody be aware that on July 4 you will start having to [pay] duties. . . . And we had a whole bunch of little importers who suddenly realized "Oh, my God, I don't know how I'm going to find this money to pay these duties. I haven't paid these duties forever." And for some people, the amount of money they were going to have to pay was their margin on the products. I mean, this was *taking away* their profit. This was a very fast way to get people real upset.

Coalition members responded to an incentive package of information and expressive/purposive benefits. Core members focused on reinforcing the magnitude of the threat while minimizing the work level required for coalition members to participate effectively.

We sent back lists of members [of Congress] that they should call with their phone numbers and fax numbers. . . . Weekly bulletins on "What's happening on GSP?" so people felt like they were included in all that kind of stuff—all this wonderful exciting inside-the-Beltway stuff. But the bottom line was, "It's coming. You're going to have to pay." And in fact it did expire. People are paying those dues right now.[5]

The coalition received a substantial infusion of membership when the GSP actually expired on 4 July 1993. Coalition members and all the free riders who had been willing to let other importers get involved found themselves paying substantial customs duties.

In the case of GSP, in the midst of this, the bad stuff *really did* happen to them. . . . [W]e had been saying, "The sky is going to fall, the sky is going to fall," and then the sky fell on July fifth. And you can imagine what happened on July sixth. Here on my phone, I mean, we got ninety phone calls from people saying, "What do I do?"

The Role of Technology

When interested companies contacted the coalition brokers with an inquiry, they were processed through the latest database technology. Secretaries took their names and fax numbers, and they were added to a database of coalition members in the broker's PC. From that initial inquiry, the coalition broker would fax out a series of memos and information notices to stimulate active participation in the coalition.

> All you had to do was call up and get your name put on my [computer's] fax board. We used the fax and we sent out these memos—these hysterical memos to people—pushing the panic button and getting them to write their own letters. And it was a small but crazed group of individuals who cared about this little tiny provision. . . . I've done this two or three times now—very successfully on some very small trade issue. You find an issue that people get very emotional about. An issue that is small so you are not competing with other groups who are competing for the attention of this small but crazed group and you make it very inexpensive for them to be a part of the coalition.

The importance of technological developments to the coalition-building process can best be seen by comparing earlier attempts at coalition formation in the international trade community with the GSP coalition. Some of the core members of the GSP coalition were able to provide a direct comparison that indicated not only the magnitude, but the speed of development.

Five years earlier, in 1988, several of the core members of the GSP coalition had put together a similar grassroots coalition to fight what was known as the "scofflaw provision" in the 1988 trade bill. The scofflaw provision was a set of customs penalties, the international trade equivalent of "three strikes and you're out" criminal penalties. As a member of the scofflaw coalition recalled it, "It was a penalty provision that could literally put you out of business. Three violations of the customs law—even clerical errors—and you lose the right to import. That was what the scofflaw penalty was. It was a stupid provision. . . . This was a coalition waiting to happen."

Like the expiration of the GSP provision, the scofflaw provision was a direct economic threat to many members of the trade community. The venue for action was remarkably similar. A trade association executive described the issues this way: "Similar issues. I mean, little tiny trade bills—trade provisions in giant, gargantuan 300-ton gorilla legislation." In both cases, a coalition built by customs brokers, attorneys, and groups representing importers was able to generate a large quantity of grassroots mail on a customs provision, but the effort in 1993 benefited by the advances in technology. One of the core players on both coalitions noted how technology had simplified the coalition building process.

> [Like the 1993 GSP coalition, on the 1988 scofflaw provision] we were able to generate tons of mail. But I didn't have the technology then. It took

hours and hours on the phone. .... And we were able to generate just a ton of mail on that particular thing, but we had to do it by telephone, which meant somebody had to spend twenty minutes explaining it to everybody. You had to do it one by one by the telephone and if you faxed stuff—we did have faxes in '88 but you had to sit there and feed papers into the thing. And we used it. It was the first time I ever used a fax. It was very effective and I thought the technology was great. But not like now. I have a fax board attached to my computer. I push a button, I send 300 faxes. And everybody has a fax machine now, particularly people who do international trade, because that is how they communicate. They either communicate on e-mail and faxes. I mean, to overseas gets there much faster than mail or any other phone.

Reaching potential coalition members, providing them with an incentive package to join, and stimulating grassroots mail campaigns were vastly simplified through technological development. Technology lowered both financial and labor costs of the brokers, and additionally, the technology allowed potential members to participate at a minimal cost to themselves.

Washington representatives seem to have a high opinion of the efficacy of technology for coalition building. The ability to attract, inform, and mobilize previously unknown companies into a large coalition within a matter of a few weeks underlines the representatives' enthusiasm.

I see a real implication for coalitions—particularly grassroots coalitions, bootstrap coalitions—through technology. .... We had three hundred-some odd members of this coalition. [It] didn't cost anything to be a member. We don't have the addresses of these people. All we have is their phone and fax number.

These kinds of short-term guerrilla coalitions, I think, are with us to stay. I think they are going to be a new fixture of American politics in my judgment. And I think we are going to see more and more of this ability to generate sort of instantaneous mail.

The Activities of the Coalition Leading to Victory

GSP Coalition brokers strove for diversity in their coalition to make their appeal seem more democratic. Since they made their initial appeals through a wide range of customs brokers and attorneys with clients scattered throughout the country, the coalition developed a widely distributed membership.

We got . . . farmers writing, and we had big electronic firms like Xerox and Motorola writing, and we had the automobile companies writing, and then we had little importers of wood and little importers of jewelry and little importers of melons and little importers—we are talking all sorts of different products.

In both the GSP and the scofflaw cases, the trade coalitions won impressive victories through inundating representatives with mail.

And it got so bad that the GSP coalition tied up Rostenkowski's lines with phone calls. I mean members of Congress—and Rostenkowski had his staff call back to the toy manufacturers and say "shut the f*** up." It was in my bill go pick on Moynihan. Well, we are picking on Moynihan—in fact, it turned out that the Senate staffer last Monday—I called—and said "Well, are you guys going to agree to this stuff or not?" He said, "Will you just shut up? Will you just stop the mail? Stop writing. We'll take care of it."

Take care of it they did. The GSP extension was approved by the House of Representatives, and went on to become law, gaining not only another year of duty-free protection for the coalition members but also a refund of duties paid during the period of GSP lapse.

The GSP Coalition not only demonstrates the manner in which core members were able to develop a successful coalition on a minimal budget but also shows the manner in which technological developments such as the use of fax board equipped personal computers simplify the task. Group representatives in the core found their investment of time and energy paid off for their own organizations. One of the founding core members of the GSP Coalition explained, "Basically I have already paid the freight for this GSP coalition. [I] won a huge victory for [my organization's] members—saved our members a lot of money . . . working through people who were not our members."

TECHNOLOGICAL DEVELOPMENT AND THE "VIRTUAL" COALITION

The technologies in use today, such as the PC databases and fax boards used by the GSP coalition, represent only the tip of the iceberg among the tools available to coalition brokers. The most fundamental development is the worldwide growth of the Internet. In the United States alone, a major study indicated that there were over 57 million Internet users in early 1998, with seventeen thousand new users going on-line every day.[6] Akin to a cyber baby boom, the first generation of computer-literate citizens is coming on-line. This trend will not reverse itself, and there are tremendous implications not only for politics as a whole, but specifically for interest groups and coalitions.

Two areas of technological innovations related to the Internet will further enhance the ability of coalitions to mobilize and respond to legislative developments at speeds approaching "real time": enhanced communications technology and expanded information availability. Although these two trends are generally known to the academic community, it is not clear that political scientists have recognized the full potential these developments have for changing the nature of coalition building among organized interests. Changes in communications technologies allow the classic process of mobilizing the grassroots for action to proceed at hitherto inconceivable speeds.[7] The exponentially enhanced availability of information, the second trend, actually changes the dynamic of interaction among coalition members, potential members, and the government.

Communications Technology

As noted above, facsimile transmission of data has the advantage of almost instantaneous information transfer. Quantities of information can be transmitted from one party to another (or others) over telephone lines much faster than the message could be spoken. One Washington representative explained, "With a fax you can communicate instantaneously with [coalition members], giving them instructions on how to call, phone and fax and otherwise get communications back to the hill." The development of the fax board for the desktop PC gave coalition brokers the ability to simultaneously initiate large numbers of fax transmissions via high-speed modems. Eliminating the need to hand-dial and hand-feed messages substantially reduced the number of man-hours required to disseminate information widely.

Given the increasing popularity of electronic mail coupled with electronic scanners, however, the fax itself may soon be obsolete. Costs for information transfer via electronic mail are truly minimal. The long-distance phone bills required for fax transmissions as well as the postal fees are being reduced drastically for many groups. Furthermore, there is a distinct economy of scale for the most active flat-rate Internet subscribers, as the piece price for e-mail services falls. As one coalition broker in the transportation sector touted the cost-efficiency of e-mail communications, "If you want to do a grassroots coalition—you can't [even] say it's going to cost you a hundred bucks, [because of] the technology—it's a technology thing here too. I have to tell you I am a real technology [fan]—I just love technology. Technology is great."

While some coalitions have embraced electronic mail communication fully, a significant number resist its use for sensitive messages because of security concerns. Though numerous software and hardware tools exist for encryption, the lack of a single standarized method remains a hindrance.

Information Availability

The second general category of technological development that is affecting the shape of coalitions is expanded information availability. Perhaps more significant, the transformation of the Internet from a mechanism for e-mail and ftp data transfer to an easily accessible, easily navigable information source is dramatically decreasing the cost of legislative information. The World Wide Web (WWW), the fastest-growing and most visible side of the information superhighway, is making government data available at rates that boggle the imagination.

The confluence of technological innovation, development, and the election of self-professed "techno-wonks" Bill Clinton, Al Gore, and Newt Gingrich to head the executive branch and the House of Representatives moved the United States government to the head of the information-distributing pack. For example, the House of Representatives initiated a WWW site named "Thomas," after Thomas Jefferson, which makes available the day-to-day status of all bills, searchable by bill number, keyword, or text word.[8] The effect that this has on information costs is staggering. Group representatives can do real-time searches of legislation for keywords of interest to their organization, and the Thomas database can identify even newly introduced legislation of relevance, whether the provision of interest is underscored in the title of the bill or "hidden" in a previously obscure footnote in a tangentially related subparagraph. The computerization of data and its ready accessibility are rendering the terms "obscure paragraph" and "hidden provisions" obsolete. Group representatives can obtain the text of amendments on the same day, peruse committee reports, and electronically search the *Congressional Record* or the *Federal Register*, regardless of where they are (and without the cost of purchasing a document subscription).

The Web itself is growing at a staggering rate. One estimate indicates that the number of Web pages doubles every 100–125 days and placed the number of Web pages at 150 million at the end of 1997.[9] A 1998 article notes that in 1993 "there were two commercial (.com) Web sites; today there are more than a million."[10]

World Wide Web sites are not only important sources for government information, but they serve as one of two important technological springboards for coalition formation and maintenance. Web sites have been created to establish a presence on the Internet for dozens of political coalitions such as the Coalition for Networked Information, the American Arts Alliance, the Wireless Opportunities Coalition, the Coalition for Vehicle Choice, United States Industry Coalition, National Coalition Against Censorship, and ACTION (ACTIvism ONline). Below the coalition level, there are already hundreds of political groups and corporate political interests represented on the Web, not to mention over 400,000 companies transacting business over the Web.[11] The growth of coalition sites on the Internet has reached the point where it has even spawned on-line parodies, most notably the "Coalition to Ban Dihydrogen Monoxide."[12]

Government affairs firms like the Wexler Group and Podesta Associates have established sites on the web. Commercial ventures such as INCONGRESS are springing up to provide one-stop information shopping for policy entrepreneurs, legislators, and lobbyists alike. INCONGRESS brings together the text of legislation and the policy position papers of organized interest groups and coalitions in one site. Organizations such as Arco, BellSouth, the Interstate Natural Gas Association, and the Career College Association have paid some $6,000 to post their position papers on the site as "charter advocates."[13] Other Washington area firms, like Net.Capitol and Capitol Advantage sell groups and coalitions software that enables their members to funnel grassroots e-mail directly to the appropriate congressional offices.[14]

A second, potentially more wide-reaching springboard for grassroots coalition formation is the set of Usenet newsgroups. Newsgroups serve as self-selecting pools of interested potential members for groups and coalitions. So far, the chief use of newsgroups by coalitions has been as a tool for generating grassroots mail. In a sense, coalitions use the newsgroups much like direct mail. The coalition broker posts a message to a newsgroup just as he or she might have sent out mailings through the postal service on other occasions.

One of the first effective uses of newsgroups by a coalition was organized in 1995 by the Campaign to Stop the U.S. Communications Decency Act. This coalition joined traditional civil liberties groups such as People for the American Way and the ACLU with newer, computer-oriented organizations such as the Electronic Frontier Foundation and Voters Telecommunications Watch. The coalition posted announcements on newsgroups such as alt.activism, alt.censorship, and alt.politics.datahighway, encouraging readers to contact members of the Senate Commerce Committee. Members of the committee were listed along with phone numbers and a list of points to make in opposition to the bill.[15]

Newsgroups bring three advantages to the political realm. First, only one posting in the form of an electronic mail message needs to be sent to reach potentially millions of recipients.[16] Second, the cost of that posting is, in real terms, reckoned in pennies. Third, the connection to potentially interested parties is made entirely without the need to obtain their names, addresses, or personal information. The only address needed is that of the newsgroup itself. People subscribe to newsgroups on the basis of their own interests, so announcements posted to a newsgroup are self-targeting. There is no need to purchase or assemble a mailing list.

The ability to mobilize individuals through Internet newsgroups stimulates overall political participation. Even people who have never been involved in politics or who might never have gotten onto political mailing lists can be contacted. Certainly, this applies more to some social spheres than others, and intriguingly, along with the obvious economic bias toward those who can afford the hardware to go online, the strongest political bias obvious on the Internet goes in a conservative to libertarian direction.[17] In fact, the "Yahoo!" directory, a well-known index of World Wide Web sites, often lists more Web sites for third parties than it does Republican or Democratic Web sites.[18] This overrepresentation of nonmainstream voices indicates that the Internet has a powerful leveling effect for political participation in at least two ways, both of which are relevant to coalition formation.

Technology lowers the entry costs for group political participation. Though this may seem counterintuitive, given the $1,000 price tag on entry-level hardware, once a group has the hardware and Internet access, it can put up Internet Web sites with the same potential viewer base as any organization in the country. In other words, unlike traditional media such as newspaper, television, and radio, in which an organization would have to pay additional pricing units for each additional market it wished to advertise in, the universal market of the Internet redefines the nature of economies of scale.

Internet technology and the creation of the World Wide Web favor participation by start-up groups and by organizations that have not committed themselves to the use of other infrastructures. As John Pike, director of CyberSpace Research at the Federation of American Scientists has noted,

> [C]onsider the dynamics of the net. In general, this new infostructure privileges those who were marginalized by the old infostructure, and those who are currently privileged by the existing infostructure will be net.lagged [sic] as [they] stick to core competencies.
>
> This is why A-albionic Research has major net.presence [sic]. The Brookings Institution is just barely venturing onto the web with a content-poor site, and CFR will probably be the last place in Western Civilization to go online. Before the net, no one had ever heard of A-albionic, and now you just can't escape it, [whereas] CFR has been around for a long time, and is well known [more or less]. CFR has a good thing going with the

existing infostructure, what with all their face-to-face get-togethers over sherry, so why should they want to display their warez [sic] to the bootless and unhorsed via the web?[19]

Taken together, the primary effects of technology for coalition brokers are to lower the cost of monitoring politics and to lower the cost of organizing a coalition. The secondary effects of these developments are to simplify the work of coalitions brokers and simultaneously to render active brokers less necessary. As noted above, the developing information infrastructure dramatically lowers the cost of monitoring governmental action. Not only is the government making information directly available to citizens via the World Wide Web, but citizens of the network—"netizens" as they sometimes call themselves—provide information to one another directly on the newsgroups and through personal home pages on the web programmed with hypertext links referring the reader to other sites of interest.[20] The lowered cost of monitoring may have the effect of depreciating the incentives for interest group leaders to join a coalition in exchange for information benefits.

The second cost that technology innovation has lowered is the cost of organizing. This is most easily seen in the new ease of like-minded potential coalition members finding one another. As Robert Wright notes about cyberspace, "The things it changes are the arbitrary constraints on interaction. Distance is not an impediment."[21] Whether this is a positive or negative development depends directly upon one's view of organized interests in American democracy. Technology overcomes one of James Madison's key protections against the rise of factions. Madison suggests in *Federalist Paper* Number 10 that an important advantage of a large republic is that like-minded individuals will have greater difficulty finding one another and organizing when they are geographically dispersed. Madison's point is moot in cyberspace.

The proliferation of electronic communications links such as Web sites and newsgroups means that interest group leaders can more easily get in touch and exchange information directly with other coalition members and interested groups. This reduces the reliance on coalition brokers as the intermediaries for information exchange.[22] Although there is no reason to believe that the core-player-peripheral structure of coalitions will change, the patterned flow of information is changing. Intermember communications are developing among all members of the coalition, expanding beyond the traditional, highly centralized channels between the entrepreneur/broker and the members.

The last way in which technology is changing the face of coalition structures is through enhancing and enabling anonymity on the part of potential coalition members. An interested party who learns about a coalition effort through monitoring a newsgroup[23] does not need to identify himself or herself to the coalition broker in order to obtain more information. In the WWW environment, an interested party does not need to make phone calls for information, does not have to leave a name, and does not have to figure out how to quietly get copies of someone else's newsletters to review for intelligence purposes. One simply examines the coalition's WWW site for information. There are obvious advantages and disadvantages of this for the coalition broker. Potential members have easy access to information, but so do potential enemies. However, current technology allows the owner of a Web site to monitor those accessing the data stored at the site. This in itself has important advantages for identifying the interested public, the first information challenge discussed in chapter 5.

The relationship between organized interests and technology can be characterized with a simple theme: potential utility begets adaptation and use. As technologies emerge, the organized interests who see potential advantages through their use will adapt them to fit their needs and put them into play. As more groups connect to the Internet and begin to discover the advantages of electronic connectivity, they will learn not only that governmental data and legislative information are easier to obtain, but that personal acquaintances are forged on-line that can lead to working relationships. The Internet creates personal as well as electronic links.

CONCLUSION

Coalitions are naturally evolving as technological developments enhance the ability of coalition members to communicate and obtain information. Given the powerful incentives for cooperation among interest groups and the advantages in communications available to communications brokers, we must turn to the question of when, if ever, we should expect not to see coalitions. I turn to this question in the next chapter as I explore questions of timing, preference, and the policy arena.

7

Timing, Preference, and the Policy Arena

INTRODUCTION: WHEN GROUPS DO NOT JOIN

Incentive theory has been useful in explaining what benefits individual group leaders respond to in joining specific coalitions. It is appropriate now to turn to the policy process to examine the general question of when coalition strategies are most and least likely to be employed. At what stages in the policy process and on which activities will coalitions become the tactic of choice? Conversely, are there specific stages of the policy process or activities in which we should expect to see groups working alone?

Incentive theory traditionally argues that interest group leaders respond to external incentives in selecting their course of action. Group leaders are attempting to maximize their utility, which they may define in terms of external influence, policy goals, job security, or any of a wealth of other criteria. In this chapter I explore three hypotheses derived from incentive theory that offer explanations of when groups are likely to form coalitions or work alone.

First and most important, I will examine a reputation enhancement hypothesis and argue that it best predicts the activities groups will or will not pursue in coalitions. To a large degree, groups are most likely to choose strategies that enable them to claim credit and enhance their long term reputations by doing so. If reputation and credit claiming can be pursued best through independent action, coalitions are less likely to form.

Naturally, there are other concerns that interest group leaders have which shape their actions. I explore two of these as counterhypotheses that refine the general thrust of the chapter. The first counterhypothesis is based upon the policy timeline: groups are more likely to employ coalitions early in the policy process rather than later. This hypothesis is based upon structural assumptions regarding the American policy process. In short, it holds that groups are more willing to compromise in the legislative phase of the policy process when policy decisions are more general, knowing that the details will be ironed out in the regulatory phase of the process.

The second counterhypothesis is based on endogenous preference and priority: groups are most likely to employ coalitions on their most pressing activities. This is a resource maximization argument. It is based on the element of incentive theory that tells us that membership in a coalition brings the combined resources of many organizations to bear on legislative issues.

The central question of this chapter is not *why* groups join coalitions but rather, *when* they will choose to join or not to join. Ample evidence exists that groups do in fact respond to numerous incentives and join coalitions. And yet there are occasions when such incentives are present, but organizations choose to pursue an independent path.

This raises one of the weaknesses of incentive theory: though it has powerful instrumental and heuristic power, it has weak predictive strength. Incentive theory can explain ex ante the instrumental set of incentives a coalition broker should offer to attract coalition members, and the researcher can use incentive theory ex post to impute a concise set of incentives group leaders responded to in their decision to join a coalition. This is exactly what I have done in chapter 3. However, it is rarely used to supply information about the group leaders who do *not* join, beyond concluding that the incentive structure was insufficient to warrant coalition participation.

Of course, it is important in itself to be able to point out that there are a limited number of significant incentive categories to which groups respond. It is important to understand the differences among organizations that join coalitions for information, those that join for symbolic benefits, and those that have strategic reasons. Interviews show that there are few if any reasons offered by group leaders and representatives that do not fit into one of these incentives. However, incentive theory does not offer us an explanation for the endogenous preferences themselves or give a good ex ante sense of likely choices. When offered membership in two coalitions regarding activities that a group is interested in, why does a group sometimes join one and ignore the other? The answer lies in a combination of endogenous preferences and exogenous incentive structures, which I will explore below.

Hence the question for this chapter: given the substantial sets of incentives I have discussed to join coalitions, when are groups likely to pursue an independent course of action? If incentive theory suggests that independent action is likely when the combination of endogenous preferences and exogenous incentives produces greater utility outside coalition membership, to use the theory predictively, we must address the question of when this is most likely to occur and why.

POLITICS VS. POLICY: THE ROLE OF REPUTATION

The desire to develop and maintain a strong reputation in Washington plays a tremendous role in the decisions interest group leaders make and the actions they take in the policy process. Reputation is an important source of political capital for organized interests, and actors that seek to maximize their effectiveness in the policy process need to consider the effects of their actions upon their reputations.[1] I am using the term "reputation" here in a very specific sense: in this context reputation can be defined as *having a unique and recognized identity as a significant and legitimate voice in the policy process.*[2]

The essence of reputation building for organized interests is self-differentiation. Developing a reputation that enhances a group's political capital requires that a group distinguish or differentiate itself from the myriad of other organizations claiming power or expertise in a given policy domain. Browne's "niche theory" points out one example of how this may be accomplished: some organizations develop technical expertise in narrow policy areas, in effect carving out their own policy niche.[3] However, this is not the only manner in which a group can differentiate itself.

Among active participants in the policy arena, the process of group differentiation is best pursued by *independent* action. When policy success is achievable alone, independent action is the better strategy to enhance a group's reputation, because victory can be claimed independently; credit need not be shared with other organizations. On the other hand, there are risks. If a group acts independently and fails, it cannot pass the blame around to coalition partners. The pursuit of independent action at the cost of success is unlikely to bolster an organization's reputation for expertise or clout.

Thus, there is a tension between gaining reputation benefits through independent action and using the coalition strategies that are successful in the policy arena. Groups must weigh their desire to build reputation through independent action against the strategic incentives pointing them toward collective action strategies to achieve success in the policy sphere. Berry notes that the tension between reputation and collective action is personal as well as institutional: "The more resources an interest group devotes to coalition activities, the less it has for doing things in its own name. Interest group leaders and lobbyists have a personal stake in working to enhance their own reputation and that of their organizations."[4]

The solution group leaders adopt is to use both independent and collective strategies *but in separate arenas.* Reputation is an instrumental good, a form of political capital that is most beneficial when actually applied to the pursuit of a policy goal. While independently won policy victories may produce powerful reputations, they may also come at high risk and costs. Thus, if organizations can garner independent reputations in arenas where they do not put their policy goals at risk, they can bank capital for use elsewhere. The *safest* place to cultivate a reputation and gain recognition is outside the battlefield where the group will eventually have to bring that reputation to bear. In fact, the safest source of reputation capital is outside the debates of the legislative policy realm altogether.[5]

One important venue in which organizations can distinguish themselves from other groups is the realm of electoral politics. For years organizations have contributed assistance to candidates through financial contributions, manpower, independent advertising, and "soft money" given to the political parties with the goal of developing positive relationships with members of Congress.[6] Because incumbents are generally reelected (especially in the House), lobbyists view a contribution strategy based on supporting incumbents as the general rule rather than as a high-risk proposition.

Organizational participation in electoral campaigns is motivated by much more than a desire to see a particular candidate elected. The motivations for campaign donations have been granted such labels as "keeping communications channels open,"[7] "currying favor,"[8] or simply "buying access."[9] These labels all represent different facets of an underlying principle; they are important ways for an organization to differentiate itself from others. As David Truman notes, "interest groups operate in a hierarchy of prestige,"[10] and it appears that group self-differentiation is the key to moving up that hierarchy.[11] For example, presidential nominating conventions serve not only as the coronation of the parties' presidential nominees, but as an opportunity for lobbyists to participate in what has been termed the "super bowl of schmooze."[12] A lobbyist attending the 1996 Republican Convention for the National Beer Wholesalers Association explained, "Basically, why I'm here is to show the flag. . . . It's reinforcing my Washington presence. There's close to 15,000 lobbyists in Washington, so you have to figure out how you separate yourself from the masses. One way to do that is to be visible at the national conventions."[13]

If, as this hypothesis suggests, groups are building political capital through developing their reputations in electoral politics as well as through developing expertise in specific niches, then campaign contributions and other forms of political action in the electoral realm are really the same phenomenon as niche creation in the policy realm. Both are forms of group self-differentiation.

To summarize, Washington representatives cooperate when necessary for *policy* outcomes. Reputation enhancement stands in tension with this policy cooperation because group self-differentiation must be pursued independently. Thus, groups seek to enhance their reputations by acting alone outside the policy arena. Given the self-differentiation hypothesis, we should expect to find significantly more independent action in *political* activities (such as campaigns), where groups focus on developing their reputations. We should find more cooperation, coordination, and collective action in activities where groups are focusing primarily on affecting policy outcomes. As noted in chapter 3, groups in the policy realm want very much to show that their goals are widely shared and their policy preferences are broadly held.

The key to understanding the politics/policy distinction is differentiating between "enabling strategies" and "terminal goals."[14] Credit claiming, reputation enhancement, and group self-differentiation are the "enabling strategies" meant to enhance a group's likelihood of obtaining its terminal goals. They are ways for groups to "jockey for position" prior to the legislative race. Thus, *political activities* are strategies meant to enable later *policy activities*. Lobbying, on the other hand, is not an activity done to claim credit or to enhance one's reputation; it is not an enabling strategy. Rather, it is the terminal activity. Organizations give money in the electoral process *so that* they can lobby from a better position in the policy process later.

For the purpose of this chapter, *"political activities" are those activities that deal specifically with the selection of individuals for public office:* political endorsements for elective office, publicizing candidates' voting records, attempting to influence political appointments, campaign work, and PAC contributions. *"Policy activities" are those that are directed at shaping specific legislative or regulatory outcomes:* various forms of lobbying (influencing the drafting of legislation or regulations, supplying information about the effects of a bill on a member's district, stimulating grassroots mail to policy makers, contacting government officials) and filing suit.

With this in mind, the hypothesis can be tested from the interview data. Ranking every activity in the data set from the most collectively pursued to the most independently pursued, table 7-1 shows the pattern predicted by our self-differentiation hypothesis: across the board for all activities, groups utilize coalitions more on policy activities than they do on political activities. This pattern holds true for all domains; there is no statistically significant difference across domains for coalition use on any of these activities.

The only policy activity close to the level of political activities (the second category in the table) is testimony before Congress. The proximity of congressional testimony to the political activities is significant for two reasons.

TABLE 7-1.

Percentage of Groups Working in Coalition or Independently, by Activity

Activity	Coalition	Alone	N This Activity
Policy activities			
Filing suit or otherwise engage in litigation	78.9	21.1	71
Helping to draft legislation	51.4	48.6	107
Alerting members of Congress to effects of legislation on their home district	46.5	53.5	101
Contacting officials directly to present your point of view	46.0	54.0	113
Generating grassroots mail to influence elected officials	45.9	54.1	98
Helping to draft rules, regulations, or guidelines	44.3	55.7	97
Testifying before congressional hearings	28.5	71.5	123
Political activities			
Attempting to influence appointments to public office	27.8	72.2	79
Making public endorsements of candidates for office	22.2	77.8	18
Making PAC contributions to electoral campaigns	19.0	81.0	42
Publicizing candidates' voting records	14.0	86.0	43
Contributing work or personnel to electoral campaigns	6.3	93.8	16

Note: Some rows may not sum to 100 percent due to rounding.

First, the only occasion on which some organizations have had the opportunity to offer formal testimony has been at confirmation hearings, an event that would fall within the definition of political activities rather than policy activities. However, since the data do not allow these instances to be separated from testimony on policy topics, I have not labeled "testimony" a political activity.

The second significant observation about the proximity of testimony to the political activities in table 7-1 is that it seems to confirm the general hypothesis: groups are more likely to pursue reputation-building activities alone. It has been argued that testimony before Congress is more of a show directed by the committee than a real opportunity for groups to change the direction of policy.[15] As Berry notes, "in and of itself [testimony] is thought to be a waste of time."[16] The views of groups are generally known before they are invited to testify, and in the case of investigative or exploratory hearings, testimony is not

necessarily linked to specific public policy proposals or pieces of legislation. In many cases, testimony serves chiefly as an opportunity for
groups to put their views on the record. An executive in the auto service
industry noted: "[Y]ou've got to testify—even though sometimes the
hearing is a show. It still makes a difference because you get it on
record, and you just got [sic] to do that." The representative from a
professional association interested in the ramifications of civil rights
laws explained, "It's useful, but not critical. And it depends. We like
to do it because it raises our profile. There's the image and the profile
game. It can be useful for raising an issue, for getting something on
the record." If a group testifies alone, it can claim credit. Thus, testifying
as part of a coalition is less desirable because it means surrendering
an opportunity for self-differentiation and reputation building.

The activity most likely to be done in a coalition is "filing suit or
otherwise engaging in litigation." This fits the hypothesis perfectly.
Lawsuits are the most specifically policy-oriented of the activities examined by the survey instrument. The very nature of the suit requires a
plaintiff to bring suit under explicit provisions of the law. There are a
number of incentives that lead organized interests to pursue lawsuits
in coalitions. The costs of bringing suit can be quite high, and finding
partners to help shoulder the potential costs is an attractive proposition.
In the framework of the reputation hypothesis, it is clear that there are
reputation benefits that can be gained by winning landmark cases. The
NAACP, for example, developed an impressive reputation through
litigating some of the most important civil rights suits of this century.
However, for most groups, lawsuits are unlikely reputation enhancers.
The hidden costs of developing legal expertise in an important niche
are extremely high, and the likelihood of being able to claim credit
from a lawsuit is fifty-fifty at best. By definition, one party will win
and one will lose. For most groups, collective action is the safer and
less expensive route to pursue in the courtroom.

Sherral Brown-Guinyard and Ashlyn Kuersten report findings dealing with coalition building and amicus briefs that support this argument. In their survey of all Supreme Court cases related to civil rights
and gender issues during the Burger Court years (1969 to 1986), they
identify 131 cases in which amicus curiae briefs were submitted. They
note that in their study, 26 of the 131 cases revealed cosponsored amicus
briefs. In highly controversial cases there were numerous cosponsored
briefs; in *Regents of the University of California v. Bakke*, 438 U.S. 265
(1978), for example, 10 of the 59 amicus briefs were cosponsored. Most
interestingly, they note a connection between repeated activity and
likelihood to participate in amicus coalitions. Almost every "repeat
filer" of amicus briefs (groups that filed briefs in more than one of the
131 cases in their sample) filed a cosponsored brief. "In almost all

instances that repeat player amici participated in the Court, they also formed coalitions." [17]

If groups are likely to be able to milk an "enabling" activity for credit, they will do that activity alone. Thus, participating in elections approaches a 90 percent sure thing, because groups that support incumbents can come out ahead almost every time. Furthermore, they can claim credit with the victors they supported. The very nature of supporting candidates is to curry favor, to distinguish your group from others, and to gain access that others do not have.

Last, the data in table 7-2 reveal a difference in the relative frequency of political and policy activities: under the narrow definitions used in this chapter, most groups participate in policy rather than politics. Specifically, the mean participation rate on policy activities is 83.3 percent. The mean participation rate on political activities is 31.3 percent.

TABLE 7-2.
Percentage of Groups Participating in Specific Activities from the Survey Instrument

Variable	Participation Level[a]	Total N
Policy activities		
Testifying before congressional hearings	98.5	130
Contacting officials directly to present your point of view	96.9	129
Helping to draft legislation	86.2	130
Helping to draft rules, regulations, or guidelines	81.9	127
Alerting members of Congress to effects of legislation on their home district	80.5	128
Generating grassroots mail to influence officials	80.1	130
Filing suit or otherwise engaging in litigation	58.7	126
Political activities		
Attempting to influence appointments to public office	62.0	129
Publicizing candidates' voting records	34.1	129
Making PAC contributions to electoral campaigns	33.1	130
Making public endorsements of candidates for office	14.7	129
Contributing work or personnel to electoral campaigns	12.4	129

[a] These percentages differ slightly from those that could be calculated from table 7-1 because those recorded in table 7-1 include only the organizations from which data on coalition behaviors were collected for the activity.

This difference stems in large part from environmental constraints. Not all forms of organized interests are allowed to participate in the political (i.e., electoral) arena. The traditional tax-exempt, nonprofit 501(c)(3) organizations are specifically banned from most political activities. These organizations must differentiate themselves through other means, such as the niche development that Browne hypothesizes.

The implications of the self-differentiation hypothesis are wide-ranging. The incentives groups respond to when they participate in the political arena lead them to act independently, and this desire for self-differentiation is the key reason why building a true electoral *coalition*, in any formal sense of the word, is nearly impossible.

POLICY STAGE AND COLLECTIVE ACTION

There are, of course, other elements that can and do affect the decisions made by interest group leaders to cooperate with one another or to act independently. The first counterhypothesis for collective action grows out of a structural question: are there more incentives for groups to engage in coalition behavior earlier or later in the policy process?[18] Interest group coalitions may not be equally present at all stages of the policy process. Groups may be more involved in coalitions in the early stages of the policy process because congressional legislation is written in more general terms than regulations are. If legislation is vague, groups can form coalitions in the legislative stage even though their policy preferences are not identical. Since many of the details of public policy are inserted at the regulatory stage, there is simply more room for compromise in the legislative process. Following this line of thought, groups are less likely to engage in coalition behavior in the later stages of the policy process, where the specificity of the regulations precludes compromise. Coalitions break down at the regulatory stage as groups attempt to recover their policy losses incurred in the compromise of the legislative stage and as they address narrower concerns impacting fewer groups.

This is not a simple hypothesis to test for a number of reason. First, groups perform many different activities at different stages of the policy process. Direct comparison of *different activities* at different stages of the policy process lends itself to ambiguous interpretations. When comparing different activities, it is impossible to distinguish whether the difference in likelihood to form coalitions stems from the stage of the process or from the nature of the activities themselves.

In addressing the question of policy stage, I have focused on one activity widely performed by interest groups at two distinct stages of the policy process: attempting to shape the manner in which bills are drafted, and attempting to shape the manner in which regulations are drafted.

As table 7-3 indicates, respondents were slightly more likely to work in coalitions at the legislative stage than in those at the regulatory stage. Furthermore, though not shown in table 7-3, the percentage of groups working in long-term coalitions drops from 30.8 percent to 22.7 percent when groups move from the legislative arena to the regulatory arena. Thus, coalitions in this sample appear somewhat less prominent in the regulatory drafting stage than in the legislative drafting stage, and the coalitions that are used in the drafting of regulations tend to be less formal.

Since the differences shown in the aggregate data in table 7-3 are small and not statistically significant, these data do not provide conclusive evidence that there is a difference in coalition behavior in the interest group universe at these two stages of policy making. Yet, interest group representatives argue that there is a difference in the use of collective action at different stages of the policy process.

An individual representing an airport-related interest noted that the collective action problem facing organizations is greater at the regulatory stage than in the legislative stage:

> The legislation is the framework and it often doesn't get into great detail. That's why the regulations to implement that legislation or draft can oftentimes be more vexing than the legislation itself; even if it is a good piece of legislation, the regs can be adverse. So, when we get to . . . that [regulatory] stage, typically the parochial interest in each of the groups tends to move us into our own interests and we let the FAA figure out how to resolve the differences.

The representative continued:

> I guess when it comes down to regs, when the differences in interpretation or differences in impact would likely come up, [they] are likely to be

TABLE 7-3.
Percentage of Groups Pursuing Collective and Independent Strategies in the Drafting of Legislation and Regulation

Activity	Coalition	Alone	N
Help draft legislation	51.4	48.6	(107)
Help draft regulation	44.3	55.7	(97)

Note: χ^2 (1 d.f.) = 1.01938; prob. = 0.31267

relatively small compared to getting the overall legislation passed, and that's why we would do it more independently.

Many groups identify the regulatory arena as a place where the specificity and detail of proposed regulations drive communications and information gathering inward to membership rather than outward to other organizations. A group representing a particular faction of the educational system explained: "Usually the consulting that we do on regulatory stuff tends to be with our own membership and not with other groups, because it's usually to figure out—to try to get some information about how a regulation or a proposed regulation might affect them."

Other respondents offered a related explanation based on institutional capabilities. In chapter 3 I noted that coalition building among interest groups was actually encouraged by government institutions who desired some "precooking," "prepackaging," or "predigesting" of policy options before they began their work.[19] This seems to be more prevalent in the legislative branch than in the agencies of the executive branch. As an air industry representative explained,

> Congress we don't think is capable of dealing with a lot of disparate interests sort of picking away at their bills. They are to an extent, but . . . they have oftentimes told us, "Why don't you and the airlines and the airports get together and work out what you want and you let us know and we will take care of it for you." Whereas the executive branch is capable—more capable—of dealing with the very specific detailed interpretation of the legislation and the regs.

It should be pointed out that this movement from collective action toward independent action is not reflected in the data along the entire length of the spectrum through all four categories of action—from "in long-term coalitions," through "in short-term coalitions" and "alone, but consult friendly groups," to "alone and independently." As table 7-4 shows, the data reflect a general move not toward "alone and independently," but rather toward "alone, but consulting friendly groups," which nets a whopping 41.2 percent plurality of the groups in the regulatory stage. Despite the move toward independent strategies at the regulatory stage, most respondents find it necessary to at least remain in contact with other groups.

ACTIVITY IMPORTANCE AND COLLECTIVE ACTION

Groups do not place the same amount of importance upon various activities. A second counter hypothesis regarding when groups are

TABLE 7-4.
Percentage of Groups Pursuing Collective and Independent Strategies in the
Drafting of Legislation and Regulation

	Long-Term Coalition	Short-Term Coalition	Alone, But Consult Friendly Groups	Alone and Independently	N
Help draft legislation	30.8	20.6	27.1	21.5	(107)
Help draft regulation	22.7	21.6	41.2	14.4	(97)

Note: Expanded version of table 7.3.
χ^2 (3 d.f.) = 5.68954; prob. = 0.12773
Some rows may not sum to 100 percent due to rounding.

likely to utilize coalition strategies is based purely on endogenous
preferences. This hypothesis suggests that group leaders are most likely
to join coalitions when they are dealing with particularly *important
activities* on which they wish to bring multiple voices to bear. Under
this hypothesis, the more importance group leaders place upon an
activity, the more likely they are to pursue that activity through coalition
strategies with which they could invoke the cumulative resources of
other organizations.

I demonstrated in chapter 4 that the group leaders who are most
interested (both in breadth and depth) in an *issue* will be the core
members of coalitions, while those who are responding to symbolic
incentives tend to become peripheral members.[20] As we explore the
various stages of the policy process, we see it is possible that group
leaders are more likely to pursue coalition strategies on the *activities*
in the political process they find most important. It is reasonable to
assume that group leaders would want to maximize the chance that
important matters are dealt with in a satisfactory manner.

Operationally, this hypothesis suggests that the importance of an
activity in the policy process will be positively correlated with the
likelihood a group would pursue coalition strategies. Evidence for the
positive correlation between the importance of a political activity and
coalition behavior is mixed. I presented group leaders with a number
of political activities and asked them how important those activities
were for their organization. I then followed up with a battery of questions about the manner in which they generally carried out those tasks,
with degree of independence or collective action serving as the scale

for responses. The correlation coefficients indicating the relationship between activity importance and likelihood to pursue that activity in a coalition were calculated and appear in table 7-5. A positive correlation indicates that the more important an activity is to an organization, the more likely that organization is to use coalition strategies when doing that activity.

The fact that almost all these activities have positive correlation tends to support the hypothesis that there is a positive relationship between the importance group leaders place upon an activity and the likelihood that they will pursue those activities in coalitions; groups viewing an activity as "very important" are inclined to work in coalitions, while less important activities tend to be done alone. However, the coefficients presented in table 7-5 are generally low, indicating that the evidence is far from compelling and that there are other significant factors not included in this basic analysis. Furthermore, one of the strongest coefficients ("helping to draft regulations, rules, or guide-

---

TABLE 7-5.
Correlations between an Activity's Perceived Importance and a Group's Likelihood to Pursue that Activity through Coalition Strategies

Activity	Correlation Coefficient
Testifying at congressional hearings	.02
Helping to draft legislation	.01
Helping to draft regulations, rules, or guidelines	−.22
Alerting members of Congress to the effects of a bill on their district	.16
Making public endorsements of candidates for office	.18
Publicizing candidates' voting records	.08
Attempting to influence appointments to public office	.22
Contributing work or personnel to electoral campaigns	.09
Making financial contributions to electoral campaigns through a PAC	.17
Generating grassroots mail to influence elected officials	.00
Contacting government officials directly to present your point of view	.05
Filing suit or otherwise engaging in litigation	−.12

Note: For each activity groups specified whether the activity was "very important," "important," "not too important," or "we do not do this." Groups participating in an activity then identified whether they generally conducted that activity "alone and independently," "alone but consulting friendly groups," "in consultation with temporary coalition partners," or "in consultation with long-term coalition partners."

lines" = – .22) is negative, indicating a stronger tendency to work alone in the regulatory stage when that is a particularly important activity for them. To place these relationships into context, refer back to table 7-1. Most groups report doing most of their activities alone most of the time. Thus, the activity-importance hypothesis is mildly supported by the data, but on most activities it is clearly incomplete.

CONCLUSION

In this chapter I have examined the interplay between a group's decision to join a coalition or work alone and three factors related to the policy process. These three hypotheses (opportunities to build reputation through self-differentiation, the stage in the policy process, and activity importance) were each intended to examine and compare factors that would make the potential benefits offered by a coalition broker more or less attractive to the organization.

Each of these hypotheses, though easily falsifiable, was supported at least in part by the data collected through interviews with Washington representatives, though the primary hypothesis is clearly the most successful. The decision to join a coalition is tempered by the opportunities that a group has to differentiate itself from other groups and develop a reputation. Political activities provide a relatively low-risk opportunity for self-differentiation. Although traditional 501(c)(3) organizations are banned from the electoral arena, other organizations (that may well participate in coalitions in the policy arena) tend to work independently in the political arena to differentiate themselves from other groups. This is the reason that electoral coalitions, in any formal sense of the word, are difficult to build. Even if a broker assembles a package of benefits to offer potential members of a coalition, the desire groups have to differentiate and build independent reputations will make it a very difficult task.

Second, comparing the most similar activity conducted in both the legislative and the regulatory stages of the policy process, I found that individual groups report that they are more likely to participate in coalitions when attempting to influence the way that general laws are drafted than when trying to influence the way that the more specific regulations are drafted. Group leaders noted that several collective action problems arise at the regulatory level that are less prevalent in the legislative arena, but the differences are not statistically significant in a sample of this size.

Last, organizations are generally somewhat more likely to work together on activities that they identify as important than on those they identify as less important. This factor, however, is not a particularly robust predictor of behavior. Whereas some groups, notably those who become core members and players, may join a coalition because of the importance they attach to successfully pursuing an activity, peripheral groups may join specifically because they do not think that the activity is worth devoting extensive time to on their own.

In the next chapter, I continue this discussion of the interaction between internal preferences and environment by exploring the connection between coalition membership, a group's ideology, and the breadth of its issue agenda.

8

Environmental Constraints: Domain Diversification and Ideological Advantage

INTRODUCTION

Not all political organizations are equally likely to participate in political coalitions; some groups are simply more likely to join than others. Relatively little attention has been paid to this issue, though there have been a number of interesting recent findings. For example, Marie Hojnacki has reported that organizations with extensive past experience with coalitions are likely to continue their behavioral patterns:

> Overall, compared to those organizations with minimal experience as allies (i.e., groups indicating they join alliances on fewer than half of all issues), frequent alliance participants (i.e., groups indicating they work as part of alliances on more than half of all issues) are between 22 and 32 percentage points more likely to engage in allied activity.[1]

What is it, however, that makes some groups frequent coalition participants while others are not?

In this chapter, I explore the interaction of preferences and political environment, focusing on the impact of an organization's ideological self-identification and the degree to which an organization operates as an "externality group" in policy domains other than its own. The chapter revolves around a two-stage premise. Groups have internal preferences that lead them to be active in certain policy domains and to identify with certain ideological communities. The manner in which these preferences interact with an organization's environment makes a difference in the decisions organizations make about whether or not to join policy coalitions. In any specific decision, group leaders weigh costs and benefits to determine how best to allocate their resources, but over the long haul, a pattern emerges in which certain ideological communities have a disproportionate ability to form long-term coalitions.

108

The heart of coalition building is a symbiotic exchange between different kinds of coalition members. Though political issues may result in strange bedfellows, the most common coalition partners come from among organizations most similar to one another.[2] For example, when asked to identify the organized interests with whom he most frequently worked, the Washington representative for an aircraft manufacturer said,

> We have the General Aviation Manufacturers Association, which is about a thirty-five member organization, Cessna, Beech, Piper, Pratt and Whitney, Garrett—those kind of companies, that build either engines, airplanes, avionics, or other kinds of parts, props, for general aviation airplanes. They each have a member, and a lot of them have guys like myself in town here. And we work together with several other organizations like AOPA [Aircraft Owners and Pilots Association], NBAA (National Business Aircraft Organization) [sic], the ATA (The Airline Transport Association [sic]) are with us 'cause they get liability problems too.

Though it is understandable that similar organizations work together more frequently than those that are quite different, it raises the question whether some types of organizations are systematically disadvantaged in collective action because the groups most similar to them are poor coalition partners. Similarly, are other groups systematically advantaged in collective action because the groups most similar to them are good coalition partners?

CONSTRAINTS AND RESOURCE MOBILIZATION IN GROUP COALITION BEHAVIOR

Groups appear to join coalitions for different reasons at different levels of analysis. The most important factors encouraging coalition behavior at the macrolevel are institutional. The separation of powers, the committee structure of the legislature, and the decline of subgovernments all affect the likelihood of groups to participate in coalitions.[3] These institutional characteristics are relevant to all organizations and provide structural incentives for groups to cooperate with one another. At the microlevel, the coalition decision is akin to the collective-action question faced by individuals deciding whether or not to join an interest group. Organized by the coalition broker, group leaders base much of their decision about whether or not to join a given coalition upon the incentive structure.

However, there is also a third set of factors that have a significant impact upon a group's likelihood of participating in a coalition—namely, preference-based environmental constraints. These are limitations on potential coalition participation caused by the interaction between a group's long-term preferences and the environment in which the group operates. The two long-term preferences I will explore in this chapter are domain diversification and ideological preference.

Domain Diversification

As noted in chapter 5, when groups take a policy position on a legislative item that is considered outside their traditional policy domain, they are acting as an "externality group." Organizations that frequently act as externality groups in a broad set of issue domains cannot maintain the expertise or the political capital to act independently in each of them. Coordination and cooperation with other groups are necessary, and that means participation in some form of coalition. I will argue that the broader an organization's policy interests are, measured by the number of issue domains their policy interests touch upon, the more likely they are to participate in coalitions.

Ideology

Second, I explore the ideological roots of coalition politics. Some organizations, by the very way in which they self-identify, become more attractive coalition partners for other organizations that cultivate similar identities. Organizational leaders bring ideological identification to their organizations. As professional activists, organizational leaders are generally more ideological than their members, and their general preferences may limit the number of groups that an organization allies itself with in Washington.[4] The manner in which organizational representatives portray the group on an ideological scale is, in fact, a significant predictor of group behavior. In this look at the role of an organization's ideological identification in shaping coalitions, I test the hypothesis that the different resources available to organizations will actually cause groups identified as conservative to have different coalition building patterns than middle-of-the-road groups or liberal groups, and vice versa.

DOMAIN DIVERSIFICATION AND COALITION USAGE

Among groups that join coalitions for strategic policy goals, one of the most important predictors of whether collective action is desirable or not is the degree to which cooperation with other groups is a cost-effective allocation of resources. Joining coalitions can be a simple way to multiply an organization's otherwise limited resources.

Hojnacki makes an important argument that the effects of such resource allocation are calculated differently for groups with a narrow interest on an issue than by groups with a broader interest on that issue. On a given issue, organizations with narrow concerns are less likely to join a coalition than those with broader concerns on the same issue: "Compared to organizations whose issue concerns are narrow, the likelihood of engaging in allied activity is between 16 and 24 percentage points higher for groups with more generic issue interests."[5] Hojnacki bases her view on the assumption that groups with a narrow concern on a given issue can best pursue their interests alone, rather than allowing their interests to be diluted in a coalition: "When a group's interest in an issue is narrow, its time and effort is better spent working alone. This is consistent with William Browne's idea that some organizations create 'issue niches' so that their interests are so specific as to not overlap with other groups."[6]

In developing his niche theory, Browne offers evidence that the agricultural groups he labels "multipurpose organizations" or "generalists" are more likely to participate in coalitions than agricultural interest groups with narrow interests.[7] Specifically, he notes that while generalists make up "only 15 percent of the instrumental players in the agricultural policy domain, this type of interest group (sometimes having most of their issue interests outside the domain) held more than 30 percent of the informal memberships in the numerous coalitions that they had joined."[8]

David Knoke also suggests that there is a positive relationship between coalition formation and "the number of domains in which an association operates."[9] My data suggest that Browne, Hojnacki, and Knoke are on the right track, and in fact, the relationship between breadth of interest and intergroup cooperation goes far beyond the decision of an organization to join a specific coalition on a given issue.

With the decline of subgovernments and the growth of relatively permeable issue networks, the number of organizations that function as externality groups within multiple policy domains is on the rise. There is a significant challenge for groups that deal with a wide range of policy areas. For an organization working alone, expertise is a costly commodity to acquire. As the number of policy domains in which an organization is active increases, the cost of acquiring expertise in each domain increases proportionally. However, expertise over a broad range of issues can be *borrowed* through membership in coalitions.

The essence of coalition politics is the sharing of resources and a division of labor. Not all organizations share equally, to be sure, as organizations may play one of three different roles in a coalition. Core groups lead and direct the coalition, often footing disproportionate costs. Specialist groups often join a coalition to shape its agenda by piggybacking a particular concern onto the broader coalition platform, while peripheral groups tag along with the crowd for symbolic benefits, such as the ability to demonstrate action to a constituency without expending significant resources. Core members may contribute the bulk of the funding, labor, and domain-specific expertise, whereas peripheral groups may lend only their name to the effort. But a satisfactory exchange relationship depends upon each of these.

According to this logic of *borrowed expertise*, organizations that are drawn into policy activities in several issue areas are most likely to be at a relative disadvantage when functioning as externality groups in issue domains other than their own, especially when compared with organizations with a home court advantage. Externality groups are often dependent upon external expertise and collaboration. Extending the structural model of coalitions presented in chapter 4, externality groups take on the role of specialists in coalitions in their attempt to influence the eventual outcome while taking advantage of the resources of the core members. One can posit the research hypothesis that group leaders who identify many issue areas as particularly important to their organization are likely to rely on coalitions more than organizations with a narrower range of interests.

To test this hypothesis, representatives were presented with a show card indicating seventeen major policy areas, and they were asked to indicate which issues were *particularly* important to them.[10] Groups were also offered an opportunity to identify issue areas not on the card that were particularly important for their organization. These issues were recorded, and the aggregate number appears in the left column of tables 8.1 through 8.3. Representatives were also asked to indicate the importance to their organization of participation in long-term coalitions, short-term coalitions, and information-sharing meetings. As table 8-1 indicates, groups that are active in multiple-issue domains are more likely to utilize long-term coalitions and to find these coalitions important than groups with a narrower set of issues.

The data on short-term coalitions also support the hypothesis. Groups that are active in more issues are more likely to take part in short-term, one-time coalitions (see table 8-2). In fact, none of the groups identifying eleven or more issue areas as important to them reported that they did not participate in one-time coalitions, whereas over 55 percent of those organizations labeled one-time coalitions "very important."

These data are consistent with the views of both Browne and Hojnacki and represent a more generally applicable finding, as they are not limited to a specific issue.

TABLE 8-1.
Importance of Belonging to a Long-Term Coalition of Groups with a
Common Interest
(By Percentage Responding)

	Very Important	Important	Not Too Important	Do Not Do This	N
1–5 issue domains	36.2	17.4	18.8	27.5	(69)
6–10 issue domains	51.1	31.1	4.4	13.3	(45)
≥11 issue domains	55.6	33.3	11.1	0.0	(9)

Note: N = 123, χ^2 (6 d.f.) = 13.3593; prob. = 0.03767
Some rows may not sum to 100 percent due to rounding.

Although a similar distribution of participation exists for other types of collective behavior, issue diversification is not a statistically significant predictor of all types of collective behavior. For example, respondents from organizations active in more than eleven policy domains found information-sharing meetings more important than did groups active in fewer domains. However, since most groups inside the Washington Beltway participate in informal information-sharing meetings and report them as being "very important," the differences presented in table 8-3 are not statistically significant at this sample size.

Domain diversification alone, however, is only one of the broad organizational characteristics that lie at the nexus of organizational preferences and political environment. In the next section of the chapter, I turn to the question of ideological perspective and the relationship between ideological communities and coalition formation.

TABLE 8-2.
Importance of Joining Informal, One-Time Lobbying Coalitions on Specific
Pieces of Legislation
(By Percentage Responding)

	Very Important	Important	Not Too Important	Do Not Do This	N
1–5 issue domains	29.0	21.7	31.9	17.4	(69)
6–10 issue domains	27.3	54.5	13.6	4.5	(44)
≥11 issue domains	55.6	22.2	22.2	0.0	(9)

Note: N = 122, χ^2(6 d.f.) = 19.683; prob. = 0.00315
Some rows may not sum to 100 percent due to rounding.

TABLE 8-3.
Importance of Holding Informal Information-Sharing Meetings with
Other Organizations
(By Percentage Responding)

	Very Important	Important	Not Too Important	Do Not Do This	N
1–5 issue domains	53.6	33.3	11.6	1.4	(69)
6–10 issue domains	57.8	33.3	8.9	0.0	(45)
≥11 issue domains	62.5	37.5	0.0	0.0	(8)

Note: N = 122, χ^2 (6 d.f.) = 2.00609; prob. = 0.91914
Some rows may not sum to 100 percent due to rounding.

STAFF AND ORGANIZATIONAL IDEOLOGY

Ideology and Coalition Formation

One of the premises of this chapter is that both preferences and environment matter. In this section, I explore the degree to which the ideological community with which an organization identifies can facilitate or inhibit coalition formation. The research question is whether groups within one ideological community are more or less likely to cooperate than organizations in other ideological communities.

Ideology is a complex proxy variable that is defined at the individual level through aggregating individual policy preferences. As the coherence of one's policy positions increases, the degree to which one reacts in ideological terms also increases.

The majority of organizational representatives in my sample (70.9 percent) can and do identify their groups by the traditional ideological terms "liberal" and "conservative." Representatives were asked, "Generally speaking, how would you describe your organization—as liberal, middle of the road, or conservative?" Of the 124 organizational respondents, 52 identified their group as liberal, 35 as middle of the road, and 36 as conservative; only one responded "I don't know."

To place the ideological responses into a more directly political context, respondents were also asked, "Overall, is your organization closer to the Democratic Party, to the Republican Party, or to neither party?" Of 123 observations, there were 44 organizations identifying with the Democrats, 49 with neither party, and 25 with the Republicans, with 5 "I don't knows." The distribution of ideological positions and party proximity is shown in table 8-4. Not surprisingly, there is a strong correlation between ideological identification and party identification, as shown in table 8-5. Groups that are identified by their leaders as

TABLE 8-4.
Distribution of Ideology and Political Party Identification

Ideology	Percentage	Party Identification	Percentage
Liberal	41.9	Democrat	35.8
Middle-of-the-road	28.2	Neither	20.3
Conservative	29.0	Republican	39.8
Don't know	0.8	Don't know	4.1

Note: Some columns may not sum to 100 percent due to rounding.

"liberal" organizations generally report that they are closer to the Democratic Party than to the Republican Party, while leaders of conservative groups report that they are closest to the Republican Party.

As the data below will indicate, although there is no significant difference in the ease with which conservative, liberal, or middle-of-the-road organizations form the daily *short-term* alliances that abound in Washington, leaders who identify their groups as conservative are much more likely to report ease in forming *long-term* coalitions. This is surprising, because representatives who identify their organization as liberal report a higher belief in the efficacy of coalitions and in the impact their organization has upon coalitions.

Differences between Short-Term and Long-Term Coalitions

Ease of Forming a Short-Term Coalition

Short-term coalitions are a mainstay of politics in Washington. For the purposes of this chapter, a short-term coalition can be understood as an alliance of organizations who unite to address a single issue, and after some resolution, the alliance dissolves. There is no pretext in a

TABLE 8-5.
Distribution of Ideology and Political Party Identification
(By Percentage Responding)

	Democrat	Neither	Republican	N
Liberal	74.5	25.5	0.0	(51)
Middle-of-the-road	11.4	82.9	5.7	(35)
Conservative	6.3	21.9	71.9	(32)

Note: N = 118, χ^2 (4 d.f.) = 107.59; prob. = 2.37e-22
Some rows may not sum to 100 percent due to rounding.

TABLE 8-6.
Response to Statement "Short-Term Coalitions Are Easy to Form"
(By Percentage Responding)

	Agree	Neither	Disagree	N
Liberal	86.3	5.9	7.8	(51)
Middle-of-the-road	81.3	9.4	9.4	(32)
Conservative	80.0	8.6	11.4	(36)

Note: N = 118, χ^2 (4 d.f.) = .77455; prob. = 0.94183
Some rows may not sum to 100 percent due to rounding.

short-term coalition that the alliance will institutionalize into an ongoing, standing coalition that will exist after the resolution of the immediate issue or legislative item. When asked to respond to the statement "Short-term coalitions are easy to form," groups across the ideological spectrum overwhelmingly agree (80 percent or more), regardless of ideological category.

Liberal, middle-of-the-road, and conservative organizations report no significant difference in the ease with which they form short-term coalitions. The pattern is quite different, however, when respondents were asked to discuss attempts to form long-term alliances.

Conservative Advantages in Long-Term Coalition Formation

Organizations were asked to respond to the statement "Long-term coalitions are easy to form" (table 8-7). The data reveal two things. First, it is much more difficult for any kind of organization to put together a long-term coalition than it is to form a short-term coalition. Less than half of the respondents in any ideological category found long-term coalitions easy to form.

TABLE 8-7.
Response to Statement "Long-Term Coalitions Are Easy to Form"
(By Percentage Responding)

	Agree	Neither	Disagree	N
Liberal	20.0	28.0	52.0	(50)
Middle-of-the-road	37.5	21.9	40.6	(32)
Conservative	47.2	8.3	44.4	(36)

Note: N = 118, χ^2 (4 d.f.) = 9.5808; prob. = 0.04811
Some rows may not sum to 100 percent due to rounding.

Second and more important, there is a significant and dramatic difference among the responses of group leaders with different ideological preferences. By a margin of over two to one, conservatives reported greater ease in putting together long-term alliances, with almost half of all organizations that label themselves conservative reporting that it is easy to form long-term coalitions. Only one-fifth of the groups labeling themselves liberal find it easy to form long-term coalitions. Middle-of-the-road groups fell directly between conservatives and liberals in their ability to form long-term coalitions easily. Organizations who identify themselves as conservatives enjoy a distinct advantage.

This is particularly interesting in light of the fact that it cannot be explained through belief in the efficacy of coalitions. In fact, organizations that label themselves liberal report significantly higher levels of belief in the efficacy of coalition strategies than organizations that label themselves conservative.

Ideology and Coalition Efficacy

Though a strong majority of all groups report that "coalitions are the way to be effective in politics," liberal groups are significantly more likely than conservative groups to make this claim. As shown in table 8-8, over 90 percent of the liberal groups interviewed agreed with the statement—18 percent more than conservative groups. In fact, not a single liberal group disagreed with the proposition, whereas 11.1 percent of the conservative groups disagreed. Similarly, liberal groups are significantly more likely to report that "our membership in a coalition makes a difference." Whereas 98 percent of the liberal groups agreed with this statement, only 83 percent of the conservative groups were likewise inclined (see table 8-9). Intriguingly, middle-of-the-road groups are least likely to state that their membership in a coalition makes a difference, possibly because middle-of-the-road implies a lack

TABLE 8-8.
Response to Statement "Coalitions Are the Way to Be Effective in Politics"
(By Percentage Responding)

	Agree	Neither	Disagree	N
Liberal	90.2	9.8	0.0	(51)
Middle-of-the-road	75.8	21.2	3.0	(33)
Conservative	72.2	16.7	11.1	(36)

Note: N = 120, χ^2 (4 d.f.) = 9.2161; prob. = 0.05592

TABLE 8-9.
Response to Statement "Our Membership in a Coalition
Makes a Difference"
(By Percentage Responding)

	Agree	Neither	Disagree	N
Liberal	98.0	2.0	0.0	(51)
Middle-of-the-road	75.0	18.8	6.3	(32)
Conservative	83.3	8.3	8.3	(36)

Note: N = 119, χ^2 (4 d.f.) = 11.8125; prob. = 0.0188
Some rows may not sum to 100 percent due to rounding.

of attachment to any well-defined ideological community in Washington. Whereas liberal groups are most likely to claim that coalitions make a difference in politics and that their groups make a difference in coalitions, conservative groups are twice as likely to form a long-term coalition easily. Why is this?

WHY LONG-TERM COALITIONS ARE EASIER FOR CONSERVATIVES TO FORM

Conservative organizations find it easier to form long-term coalitions for the same reason that conservative organizations are generally thought to have a dominant role in politics: the universe of conservative organizations holds the lion's share of business interests and as a result is disproportionately endowed with the resources that facilitate political action. These include monetary resources, political action committees, staff with government experience, access, and, I would argue, *organizational members*.

Self-identified conservative organizations in my sample were composed primarily of just three groups: firms, trade associations, and professional associations. Indeed, taken together, these resource-rich categories account for over 80 percent of the conservative organizations in the sample.

The financial resource advantages available to organizations that label themselves conservative are formidable and well known. Indeed, these organizations are said to hold a privileged position in American politics by virtue of their role in the economy and their financial resources.[11] For example, as table 8-10 shows, conservative organizations are more than twice as likely as liberal organizations to have an affiliated political action committee (PAC). The implications of this concentration

TABLE 8-10.

Percentage of Organizations with an Affiliated PAC

	Have PAC	No PAC	N
Liberal	23.1	76.9	(52)
Middle-of-the-road	22.9	77.1	(35)
Conservative	55.6	44.4	(36)

Note: N = 113 χ^2 (2 d.f.) = 12.3072; p. = 0.00213

of financial resources among conservative organizations are quite important for our understanding of the ideological component of coalition building. Financial resources are one of the key elements required of core members in a coalition.

Coalition formation depends upon a coalition broker's ability to mobilize resource-rich organizations to form the nascent coalition's core membership. The disproportionate accumulation of resources among conservative organizations enables them to fulfill this core function more easily than organizations from less well-endowed communities. The more groups there are that are capable of being effective core members—e.g., supplying the needed resources—the more likely that community is to report ease in forming coalitions.[12]

The resource advantages of conservative organizations are not limited solely to the financial resources at their command. The second key resource for coalition building is found in the type of membership that conservative membership associations have. Whereas liberal membership associations tend to be composed of individuals, the vast majority of conservative associations have organizations as their members. As table 8-11 shows, two-thirds of the organizations that label themselves liberal rely on individual membership; this is twice the rate we find

TABLE 8-11.

Percentage of Groups with Individuals as Members

	Have Individual Members	No Individual Members	N
Liberal	64.0	36.0	(50)
Middle-of-the-road	45.5	54.5	(33)
Conservative	33.3	66.7	(27)

Note: N = 110, χ^2 (2 d.f.) = 7.1587; prob. = 0.02789

TABLE 8-12.

Percentage of Groups with Organizations as Members

	Have Organizational Members	No Organizational Members	N
Liberal	38.8	61.2	(49)
Middle-of-the-road	66.7	33.3	(33)
Conservative	81.5	18.5	(27)

Note: N = 109 χ^2 (2 d.f.) = 14.5421; prob. = 0.0007

among groups that label themselves conservative. The other side of the coin is shown in table 8-12, where the data indicate that more than four-fifths of the organizations identifying themselves as conservative organizations have organizational members, while slightly more than one-third of the self-identified liberal organizations do. Conservative groups gain a key advantage for coalition building through their reliance on organizational memberships. An organizational member can mobilize more political resources (such as monetary resources, staff, manpower, technical expertise, and experience) than most individual members can. In an extreme example, corporate or organizational memberships in an association provide an instantaneous ability to form an apparent coalition simply by establishing a new, strictly political forum in which the same members can meet under a new name. This facilitates the task of finding a core membership, and establishing the coalition core is the central hurdle for the coalition broker to get over. This coalition can then be expanded as new specialist groups and peripheral members join the existing core.

CONCLUSION

Organizations do not operate in a vacuum when they make their decisions about whether or not to join coalitions. In addition to the specific factors related to the particular policy issue at hand, groups exist in a political environment that is shaped by their actions and preferences. In this chapter I have suggested that our understanding of coalition behavior must take this interaction between preferences and environment into account.

Organizations that choose to participate in debates outside their home policy domain are different from groups that are playing on their own home court: externality groups are often plagued by an information disadvantage. Given the high cost of developing expertise in multiple policy domains, there is a strong incentive for externality groups to join coalitions in the role of a specialist. From within the coalition, they may attempt to shape the broader coalition platform, while "borrowing" expertise from other groups native to that policy domain. The more policy domains a group is active in, the more likely that group is to rely on coalitions.

A second area of study in this chapter was the role of ideological preferences. Though liberal groups stress the importance of coalitions more than conservative groups do, conservative groups are able to form long-term coalitions more easily than liberal groups. This is due largely to the disproportionate resources available to the conservative community. In essence, a random group with conservative preferences has a systemic advantage because the organizations with these ideological preferences are better coalition partners. Their resources make them more capable of carrying out the roles of a coalition core member.

The substantial resource advantages conservative organizations enjoy provide liberal groups with a strong incentive to form long-term coalitions. This was reflected in table 8-8. The irony is that these same resource advantages make it easier for the conservatives to form long-term coalitions of their own.

9

Political Coalitions in America

INTRODUCTION

Coalitions are ubiquitous, and for good reason. Interest group politics is the politics of collective action, not only on the individual level but also on the organizational level. In a fragmented political universe without central actors dominating policy spheres, there are strong incentives leading organized interests to ally themselves with other organizations in pursuit of their policy goals.

My goal in this project has been to explore coalition building among organized interests and through that to deepen our understanding of interest group interaction and issue networks. It would be incorrect to suggest that issue networks are merely composed of several coalitions. Coalitions are no respectors of the issue networks concept; the increasing prevalence of externality groups in policy debates and the old saw about strange bedfellows point away from those conclusions. Coalitions are the operating conduits for intergroup action. Networks, on the other hand, do not "do" anything.

This exploration of coalition strategies among organized interests has developed several important themes dealing with the strategic choices Washington representatives make. In this concluding chapter I will review the research contained in the book and consider some of the implications of coalition proliferation on American political life.

SUMMARY OF RESEARCH

The Decision to Cooperate

When trying to understand the reasons group leaders and representatives join coalitions, it is very helpful to approach the problem through the framework of exchange theory. Like the members of interest groups who respond to selective incentives in their decision to join a group, coalition members join in exchange for benefits as well. However, the specific incentives that coalition members respond to differ slightly from the selective benefits Robert Salisbury describes at the group level. Washington representatives generally join coalitions for three primary reasons: strategic incentives, selective information benefits, and symbolic benefits.

The collective action problems coalition brokers face are different in several important ways from the collective action dilemmas faced by interest group entrepreneurs. First, the potential members of a coalition are Washington representatives who do not operate in a prepolitical state. Where Mancur Olson's Logic and Salisbury's Exchange Theory described potential members who needed to be induced into political action, policy advocacy is usually one of the defining characteristic of a Washington representative's job description. Group representatives who appear to free ride are not perceived by members or management as doing their job. Hence, group representatives *will* act on policy issues that are important to their organizations; the question is *how* they will pursue their policy goals.

There are a number of developments in the Washington political environment that create strategic incentives for collective action at the coalition level. Chief among these are the decentralization of government, the expansion of the subcommittee system, and the increase in multiple referrals of bills. Each of these generates additional work for a group representative interested in contacting the relevant decision makers on a given policy issue. Through the use of coalition strategies, the costs of political representation on an issue may be significantly reduced, as work and resource demands are spread across multiple actors.

Second, the increase in the number of interests represented in Washington pushes organizations toward coalition strategies. The increasingly complex and multifaceted demands on American political institutions have led policy makers in many cases to propose that groups predigest and prepackage their policy demands, in effect working out some of the kinks before approaching policy makers. As coalitions develop to assimilate demands, a strong incentive for membership in the coalitions emerges; groups who do not participate in these coalitions may find their interests overlooked or ignored.

A third strategic component in the adoption of coalition strategies is the widespread belief among Washington representatives in the efficacy of coalitions. As noted in chapter 3, many group representatives and leaders believe that they will lose their ability to shape the outcome of issues if they do not participate in coalitions.

Not all groups are responding to strategic incentives when they join coalitions. In fact, many organizational representatives join political coalitions to access the flow of information that exists in the coalition environment. Given the importance of timely information at all stages of the policy process, access to new sources of intelligence is a general requirement for group representatives.

Other group representatives join coalitions for symbolic reasons, primarily as low-cost activity trophies that they can present to their superiors to bolster evaluations or to their members for group maintenance purposes. Participation in coalitions serves as a way to demonstrate activity in the policy world, whether or not there is a significant expenditure of resources or effort aimed at achieving some sort of terminal political goal. The use of coalitions to create the illusion of significant activity is made possible by the information asymmetry known as the principal-agent problem.

Coalition Structures

The incentives group representatives respond to in joining a coalition are interesting for our understanding not only of coalition brokerage but also of coalition organization, leadership, and the ongoing relationships among coalition members. Members who have high levels of general interest about legislative proposals are likely to respond to strategic incentives in joining a coalition. They perceive coalition membership as a way to further their policy agenda through a collective approach. The groups that pursue overall strategic victory are likely to emerge as the core members—the leaders and heavy hitters—of a coalition. These are the organizations that invest the lion's share of time and other resources in the coalition effort.

Coalition members who have a narrower issue focus and demonstrate a high interest in specific sections of legislation are likely to join coalitions in order to hone the coalition agenda to include their particular spin on the legislation. These players bring their specialized expertise to the coalition in exchange for the opportunity to piggyback their legislative agenda onto the broader coalition platform, and their commitment of resources is closely tied to their narrow agenda. If these specialists are unable to shape the coalition agenda from within, they are likely to leave the coalition rather than continue to supply resources to an unprofitable exchange.

In the calculus of interest group membership, the selective benefits that Olson and Salisbury discuss are geared at convincing free riders to ante up membership dues rather than simply waiting for the collective benefits to flow. In the logic of political coalitions, would-be free riders are often encouraged to join a coalition as peripheral members without any expenditure of material resources. The cost of membership may be simply granting the coalition the right to use the peripheral group's name.

The selective benefits enjoyed by these peripheral members are often purely symbolic, perhaps only the ability to report to interested parties that they are members. The exchange between the core members and these peripheral members of the coalition is quite significant. Groups responding to symbolic incentives or for information benefits are unlikely to supply the group with any significant material benefits. Rather, their presence and the use of their name are the primary resources they offer in exchange for membership. Core members accept these peripheral members, because of the perception that there is strength in numbers. Every group that signs onto a petition lends an air of both strength and legitimacy to the general policy demands of the core members.

Intergroup Links

Organizations do not exist in a vacuum, and coalitions do not form out of one. Hugh Heclo based his model of an issue network on a conception of transient relationships emerging from shared interest or expertise. I have suggested that there are long-standing relationships based on institutional links in addition to those based on ideas. In fact, every organization is linked to other organizations through a loose web of institutional relationships such as shared board members, outside attorneys and lobbyists, and crossed career paths.

Each of these links is a source of information about other organizations, their political preferences, and their likely actions in a policy arena. As such, these links help potential coalition members overcome information problems. Information about other groups, as well as their policy preferences and activities, is the lifeblood of political organizations. Without it, trying to plan a coalition strategy is akin to piloting a plane through twisting valleys without a map.

Of the many institutional links between groups, the most significant is the one-way door of experience through which staff members move as their career takes them from organization to organization. Rather than a system of revolving doors, in which one might expect reciprocal communication and benefits between current and former employers, this study has shown that information and experiential benefits flow overwhelmingly in one direction. Group leaders report that their staffs serve as important contacts to their former employers and that these contacts are important in coalition building. From the perspective of former employers, however, staff members who leave are not considered particularly helpful coalition contacts. In many cases, the activities and preferences of the new employer remain a gray box to the former employer, and contacting former staff members carries the risk of mobilizing the opposition.

This is not to suggest naively that all coalitions, or even most coalitions, are formed by group representatives calling up their former employers. Rather, it is to identify an important link—a link that group leaders themselves identify as important—that has been overlooked often in earlier works on coalition building. Information is a crucial prerequisite for coalition building, and institutional links are as reliable a source of information as one could hope for.

Communication and Technology

The steady flow of information is no less crucial for coalitions after they are operational than it was when they were starting up, and coalition brokers today have distinct advantages over their counterparts of a generation ago. With the continuing advance of computer-based technologies, communication is easier in at least three key ways.

First, personal computers can now effectively manage mass information flow for coalition members in a fraction of the time required a decade ago. The linkage of fax technology to the personal computer allows for the speedy and unsupervised delivery of information at any time of day or night. Second, the growing popularity of electronic mail, the ability to deliver attachments with electronic mail, the increasing simplicity of graphical interfaces, and the cost advantage electronic mail enjoys over the fax for long-distance transmission bring advantages of their own.

Last, the Internet is becoming a significant tool for grassroots coalition brokers as they experiment with recruiting members through Usenet newsgroups and post their position papers, advertisements, and newsletters on the World Wide Web. Electronic communication reduces the transaction costs for coalition brokerage and maintenance.[1]

Policy and Politics

Despite the potent combination of incentives, institutional links, and enabling technologies, groups do not coordinate all activities. The desire to join a coalition is tempered by the need for groups to differentiate themselves from one another and to develop independent reputations as significant and legitimate voices in their own right.

Groups appear to join coalitions to pursue their policy goals somewhat more frequently in the legislative arena than in the regulatory arena, and somewhat more frequently on activities that are important to them than activities that are less important to them. However, the biggest differences in the level of coalition activities arise in the chasm between policy activities and political activities. In the policy arena, strategic and selective incentives lead groups to coordinate their actions on a wide range of activities. In the political arena, on the other hand, groups prefer to work alone to differentiate themselves from one another by assisting candidates through campaign contributions (using affiliated PACs), by supplying workers (a longtime favorite of organized labor), through favorable endorsements, and through testimony aimed at supporting or defeating an executive branch nominee. Many groups abstain from some of these behaviors, but those who participate tend to do so alone. Differentiation in the political arena can generate political capital that groups can bring with them into the policy arena where their terminal goals lie. Indeed, developing a strong identity in the political arena may make a group a more desirable coalition partner in the policy arena.

Issues and Ideology

The more issues that organizations tackle in the Washington policy arena, the more useful coalitions are to them. Organizations participate in more coalitions when they operate in multiple policy domains. For groups that are active in unfamiliar policy domains as externality groups, coalitions are a way to borrow expertise from other organizations.

Organizations' ideological and party preferences affect their participation in political coalitions as well. Group leaders that identify their organization as liberal report higher efficacy scores for collective action and coalition building than group leaders who label their organizations conservative. However, conservatives are significantly more likely than liberals to report ease in forming long-term coalitions. Since the conservative organizations are often linked to business, they can benefit either directly or indirectly from the resources that give business a "privileged position" in American politics.[2]

These ideological divisions are reflected in the distribution of business-related organizations in the three domains. Within the transportation sample three times as many organizations label themselves conservative as call themselves liberal (see table 9-1). In the education and civil rights domain, on the other hand, there were three times more self-reported liberals than conservatives in the sample.

Not surprisingly, business interests are most prevalent in the transportation domain, where firms and trade associations account for 63.3 percent of the organizations. At the other end of the spectrum, business

TABLE 9-1.

Response to Question "Generally Speaking, How Would You Describe Your Organization—as Liberal, Middle-of-the-Road, or Conservative?" (By Percentage Responding)

	Liberal	Middle-of-the-Road	Conservative	N
Transportation	14.3	33.3	52.4	(42)
Education	58.0	24.0	18.0	(50)
Civil rights	54.8	29.0	16.1	(31)

Note: N = 123, χ^2 (6 d.f.) = 24.2375; prob. = 7.2E-05
Some rows may not sum to 100 percent due to rounding.

interests amount to only 26 percent of the organizations active on education issues and 19.4 percent of the organizations active in the civil rights domain. This distribution of organizations and ideology across the domains has a significant effect upon the coalition patterns in those domains.

ISSUE DOMAINS AND COALITION BUILDING

Examining three policy domains, each with a different composition of organizational types, has given us the opportunity to explore whether the use of political coalitions differs significantly across issue areas. In some cases, it does. In the space below I will briefly summarize some of the differences in coalition behavior across the transportation, education, and civil rights domains before turning to the implications this study raises for our understanding of atomism and faction in America.

Transportation

Coalition building in the transportation domain is laced with irony. While many of the organizations active in the domain display an abundance of the resources that simplify the task of coalition formation, organizations in this domain are the least likely to identify long-term coalitions as important.

Business interests are active in the transportation domain at much higher rates than in the education or civil rights domains, and this has several implications for coalition patterns in the domain. First, compared with the education and civil rights domains, organizations in the transportation domain boast significantly more intergroup links. This can be seen in more board interlocks, more reported useful commu-

TABLE 9-2.
Response to Statement "Long-Term Coalitions Are Easy to Form"
(By Percentage Responding)

	Agree	Neither	Disagree	N
Transportation	46.8	12.8	40.4	(47)
Education	25.0	18.8	56.3	(48)
Civil rights	26.7	33.3	40.0	(30)

Note: N = 125, χ^2 (4 d.f.) = 9.49023; prob. = 0.04995
Some rows may not sum to 100 percent due to rounding.

nication through board interlocks, more reported benefits through interlocks, more useful communication through staff contacts with former
employers, and more contacts to other organizations in the domain
through their outside attorneys (refer back to table 5-13).

Second, because of these resources at their disposal, groups active
in the transportation domain are significantly more likely to report that
forming long-term coalitions is easy (table 9-2). In a domain dominated
by business interests, the economic bottom line provides a powerful
common metric for organizations to evaluate the utility of cooperation.

Though these resources may simplify the task of forming coalitions,
that does not mean that these organizations can or will maintain those
coalitions once the need of the moment is over. In fact, organizations
in the transportation domain report significantly more difficulty maintaining a long term coalition (table 9-3). The intense economic competition between firms and modes of transportation creates incentives to
limit the duration of cooperation once goals have been achieved.

In the fluid competitive environment of the transportation domain,
where coalitions can be formed easily and institutional links abound,

TABLE 9-3.
Response to Statement "Long-Term Coalitions Are Easy to Maintain"
(By Percentage Responding)

	Agree	Neither	Disagree	N
Transportation	19.1	6.4	74.5	(47)
Education	27.1	18.8	54.2	(48)
Civil rights	30.0	23.3	46.7	(30)

Note: N = 125, χ^2 (4 d.f.) = 7.9443; prob. = 0.09375
Some rows may not sum to 100 percent due to rounding.

TABLE 9-4.
Importance of Belonging to a Long-Term, Organized Coalition of Groups
with a Common Interest
(By Percentage Responding)

	Very Important	Important	Not Too Important	Don't Do at All	N
Transportation	23.9	32.6	10.9	32.6	(46)
Education	56.0	14.0	16.0	14.0	(50)
Civil rights	54.8	25.8	9.7	9.7	(31)

Note: N = 125, χ^2 (4 d.f.) = 17.3421; prob. = 0.00811

groups are significantly less likely to see long-term coalitions as important (table 9-4).

Instead, organizations in the transportation domain are more likely to stress the importance of short-term coalitions focused on specific pieces of legislation than long-term coalitions. Transportation groups place greater significance upon informal one-time coalitions than organizations in either the education or civil rights domain (table 9-5).

Civil Rights

Organizations active in the civil rights domain are unable to identify as many institutional links tying groups together as organizations in the transportation domain report. Not only did organizations in the civil rights sample report the fewest useful connections to other groups through boards of directors, but these organizations were also the least

TABLE 9-5.
Importance of Joining Informal, One-Time Lobbying Coalitions on Specific
Pieces of Legislation
(By Percentage Responding)

	Very Important	Important	Not Too Important	Don't Do at All	N
Transportation	31.1	46.7	11.1	11.1	(45)
Education	30.0	24.0	32.0	14.0	(50)
Civil rights	29.0	32.3	32.3	6.5	(31)

Note: N = 125, χ^2 (6 d.f.) = 9.795727; prob. = 0.13352
Some rows may not sum to 100 percent due to rounding.

likely to hire outside attorneys (only 50 percent). Fewer still hire outside lobbyists (just 23.3 percent), and none of the organizations that identified themselves as civil rights groups per se hired any outside lobbyists.

Whereas groups in the transportation domain tend to eschew long-term coalitions, these coalitions have played a special role in the civil rights domain for several decades. Organizations in this domain might be thought of as long-term coalition experts. Though groups in all domains agree that long-term coalitions are not as easy to maintain as short-term coalitions, only 46.7 percent of the organizations active in civil rights claim that long-term coalitions are hard to maintain, compared with 74.5 percent of the organizations in transportation and 54.2 percent in education (see table 9-3).

Organizations in the civil rights domain were also more likely than groups in transportation or education to call long-term and recurrent coalitions "important" or "very important." In part this is due to the longevity and historical success of specific coalitions. Washington representatives repeatedly mentioned specific long-standing coalitions as examples, most notably the Leadership Conference on Civil Rights. When the discussion turned to short-term coalitions, however, examples were more abstract, and fewer groups than in the transportation sample identified short-term coalitions as important.

Education

Organizations active in the education domain reported the fewest useful institutional links of any domain. Groups in the education sample reported minimal usefulness of staffer connections to former employers and were the least likely to say that interlocks were beneficial for communications. These organizations were also the least likely to know whether their outside attorneys had any connections to other groups in the domain. In fact, almost three quarters of the externality groups working on an education issue did not even know whether their attorneys had other clients in the field of education.

Only 18 percent of the organizations in the education sample hire outside lobbyists, far fewer than groups in the other two domains. Though groups active in education do hire outside attorneys, their attorneys generally do not represent other organizations in the education domain at anywhere near the rate at which attorneys in civil rights or transportation represent multiple clients in those domains.

The organizations in this sample are also the least likely to view one-time or short-term coalitions as important parts of the work that they do. In fact, 46 percent of the groups in the education domain reported that one-time coalitions were "not too important" or that they did not use them at all. However, one recent study of lobbying in higher education suggests that a change is afoot in that segment of the education domain. The study noted that groups representing colleges and universities have generally not built alliances with groups outside the education community, but it argued that an increase in the use of ad hoc coalitions took place in the 104th Congress.[3] Future research will be needed to determine whether the increase is lasting.

On the other hand, a majority of groups in the education sample identified long-term coalitions as very important. Several groups with an interest in higher education mentioned the ongoing relationship of the Big Six. Organizations involved in public education referred frequently to the Committee for Education Funding, which is active on appropriation legislation.

Universals

Despite these differences among domains, there are some behaviors that we see across all domains at similar rates. The great universal for almost all groups in Washington is the plethora of informal information-sharing meetings that get penned into calendars across the city every day. Whether these meetings are held weekly, biweekly, or monthly, this kind of event is a staple of Washington organizational life. Between 87 and 91 percent of the organizations in each of the domains labeled informal information sharing meetings "important" or "very important." Surprisingly, though organizations with a small government relations staff may be more dependent upon this type of meeting for their day-to-day intelligence, there is no statistically significant difference in reported importance based on staff size. Whereas coalitions are held together by symbiotic exchanges to achieve a set of goals negotiated by the members, information-sharing meetings often exist independent of a specific legislative agenda because everyone needs information.

Washington representatives in all three domains also agreed on the importance of general strategy meetings with other groups or firms. Strategy meetings were labeled "important" or "very important" by over three-quarters of the respondents in each domain, without a statistically significant difference among the domains.

Though there is a striking difference across domains for the ease of long-term coalition formation, the same cannot be said for short-term coalitions. Approximately four out of five organizations in each of the three domains agree that short-term coalitions are easy to form.

Although the frequency with which coalition strategies are employed varies widely by the type of political or policy activities an organization undertakes (see table 7-1), there is little evidence that the frequency or style of coalition used differs significantly by domains. Among organizations that make PAC contributions or endorse candidates, for example, those active in the civil rights domain are statistically just as likely as those in the education and transportation domains to seek to develop their reputation and identity by pursuing these strategies alone rather than in a coalition.

COALITIONS AND FACTION IN AMERICA

In this book I have taken a concrete piece of the interest group universe, the political coalition, and subjected it to careful scrutiny. Drawing from both the rich literature of interest group formation and the less bountiful literature on cooperation among organized interests, I have offered an explanation of the key factors involved in the formation, maintenance, and strategies of interest group coalitions. But what do these coalitions mean for the American political system?

The American Constitution was designed to develop specific governmental powers in a framework of institutional checks and balances. Though the business interests of K Street and the nonprofits on the Fourteenth Street corridor feel very far from the world of the Founders, their strategies today are in part by-products of the large republic Madison discussed in *The Federalist* No. 10. In that essay James Madison described the pernicious effects of societal factions, which he defined as "a number of citizens, whether amounting to a majority or a minority of the whole, who are united and actuated by some common impulse of passion, or of interest, adverse to the rights of other citizens, or to the permanent and aggregate interests of the community."[4] Madison argued that creating a large republic would control the effects of these factions by creating a more diverse society. In a republic with many factions spread over a large geographic area, it would be difficult for any single faction to dominate the political system. Governance would be conducted by a government of representatives elected by individuals as far-flung and diverse in their opinions and interests as they were in their geography. Passing any legislation would require the agreement of legislators from a plethora of backgrounds.

Societal factions, whether defined perniciously, as Madison chose, or more benignly as economic or demographic sectors, are not identical to organized interests. However, Madison's goal, expressed in *Federalist* 51, of "comprehending in the society ... many separate descriptions of citizens" foreshadows the proliferation of organized interests and the ensuing rise of interest group coalitions.[5] Whether the heavenly chorus in the pluralists' heaven sings with an upper-class accent or not, one thing is certain: coalitions are the only means by which a chorus of any kind can emerge from the cacophony of organized factions active in Washington.[6]

Coalitions of organized interests bear witness both to the difficulty of passing legislation under the American Constitution and to the diverse set of cues to which a diverse body of legislators is attentive. Though similar in their goal of reelection, individual members of Congress must pursue that goal with careful reference to the unique demands of voters in their districts.[7] This provides an incentive for a coalition broker to actively recruit members to the coalition who can appeal in a unique way to specific legislators while demonstrating breadth.

In the high-stakes battle over the renewal of China's "Most Favored Nation" trade status, aerospace giant Boeing brokered a huge grassroots coalition that took out full-page advertisements in regional papers across the country. Trying to assemble a coalition of small businesses that could appeal to particular members of Congress, Boeing approached the owner of a small doughnut shop in a supplier's plant. An airline representative summarized the situation: "This guy would probably lose his business if MFN was eliminated. They brought him to meet with his Congressman—and his impassioned appeal alone swayed the member's vote. It is the little stories that have the most impact." As coalitions pursue their agenda by bringing in a diverse set of coalition partners, they are pursuing the sometimes tedious strategy anticipated by the logic of *Federalist Papers* 10 and 51.

To the degree that coalitions of organized interests authentically represent a compromise of public views, they would appear to be a positive voice on the political landscape. There is at least some evidence that they do play a moderating role. Two-thirds of the respondents from each domain agreed that "being part of a coalition means that a group must surrender some of its independence of autonomy." However, though there are elements of compromise in every coalition, to accept such statements as evidence of Aristotelian virtue is shortsighted.

Despite the goal of creating a coalition that appears broad, inclusive, and democratic, appearance does not precisely reflect reality. The peripheral groups in a coalition tag along for symbolic benefits, and their presence partially masks the significance of the core members and the narrow parochial interests of players. The driving core of a coalition may not be obvious to outside observers. When a legislator receives a letter signed by representatives from forty-five organizations, it is difficult to assess which groups are driving the process and which names are attached to lengthen the list.

After he spent a year on the Hill as a Congressional Fellow, an acquaintance told me that he simply could not believe the coalition letters that would come into the office with dozens of signatures. He said he often wondered "what they had in common that made them all so interested in getting a bill passed." The answer suggested in this book is that they were not all so interested in getting the bill passed: the core members wanted the bill; the players wanted a paragraph; and the peripheral groups wanted a picture for their newsletter. Each lobbyist defined his or her essential interest, and a symbiotic relationship was forged.

Though it is a mistake to see coalitions as a democratic panacea and a solution to the problems of faction, there are some reassuring themes that emerge from these data. The powerful economic and political position of business has been an issue of intense interest to political scientists and sociologists, and the degree to which business is able to wield its privileged position is an important area of study. While this book suggests that business interests do enjoy certain advantages in collective action, such as interorganizational linkages, it also presents evidence that business interests and domains dominated by business groups have a more difficult time maintaining long-term coalitions. Corporations and trade associations move easily into short-term coalitions, but they are at heart competitors rather than colleagues.

CONCLUSION

In his classic essay on issue networks, Hugh Heclo sketches a political system with fuzzy boundaries and transient relationships where successfully enacted government policies propagate hybrid interests. He describes the atmosphere of exponentially multiplying groups and policies as "congestion" akin to a Paris traffic circle in which groups increasingly experience "accidental collisions."[8] The only solution for Washington representatives confronted with Heclo's traffic circle is to cope the same way factions faced with Madison's large republic do: by lobbying together.

Appendixes

APPENDIX A

Quantitative Data Variables

TABLE A-1
Quantitative Data Variable Summary
(By Category and Variable)

Category	Variable	Data Gathered
Interview parameters	V1	Organization number
	V2	Domain
	V3	Date interviewed (YYMMDD)
Organizational descriptors	V4	General category of organization
	V5	Type of firm
	V6	Type of association
	V7	Recode of organization type
	V8	Headquarters location
	V9	Date DC office established
	V10	Year founded
	V11	Ideology measure
	V12	Party organization closest to
	V13	Position on regulation
	V14	Position on social services
	V15	Issue interests
	V16	Key issue area
	V17	Percentage of time: this domain
Organizational resources	V18	Individual members
	V19	Number of individual members
	V20	Organizational members
	V21	Number of organization members
	V22	Groups: number paid staff
	V23	Groups: number government relations staff
	V24	Groups: volunteer staff
	V25	Groups: number volunteers
	V26	Groups: number full-time volunteers
	V27	Groups: number volunteers in government relations
	V28	Corporate: number employees

Organizational resources *continued*	V29	Corporate: number employees in government relations
	V30	PAC
	V31	Budget

Organizational links	V32	Board of directors
	V33	Number board members
	V34	Board links
	V35	Board link ID
	V36	Board link advantages
	V37	Board link beneficial
	V38	Board link communication
	V39	Number staff with government experience
	V40	Number staff with other organizational experience
	V41	How useful staff past links
	V42	Former staff still in domain
	V43	Former staff importance
	V44	Former staff communication
	V45	Staff past link communication
	V46	Outside lobbyists/reps
	V47	Representatives links
	V48	Name representative links
	V49	Outside attorneys
	V50	Attorney links in domain
	V51	Name attorney links

Opinions on coalitions	V52	Short-term ease to form
	V53	Short-term ease to maintain
	V54	Long-term ease to form
	V55	Long-term ease to maintain
	V56	Helps control outcome of issue
	V57	Way to be effective
	V58	Lose ability to shape outcomes
	V59	Membership makes a difference
	V60	Surrender independence/autonomy

Importance of coalition activities	V61	Strategy meetings
	V62	Informal info sharing meetings
	V63	Onetime lobbying coalitions
	V64	Re-forming lobbying coalitions
	V65	Long-term organized coalitions

| Coalition number and membership | V66 | Number of long-term coalitions |
| | V67 | Number of members in each |

| Activities and coalition use | V68 | Testifying/Congress: importance |
| | V69 | Testifying/Congress: context |

V70	Draft legislation: importance
V71	Draft legislation: context
V72	Draft regulations: importance
V73	Draft regulations: context
V74	Alert to effect on district: importance
V75	Alert to effect on district: context
V76	Public endorsements: importance
V77	Public endorsements: context
V78	Publicize records: importance
V79	Publicize records: context
V80	Influence appointments: importance
V81	Influence appointments: context
V82	Campaign work: importance
V83	Campaign work: context
V84	PAC giving: importance
V85	PAC giving: context
V86	Grassroots mail: importance
V87	Grassroots mail: context
V88	Direct contact: importance
V89	Direct contact: context
V90	Filing suit: importance
V91	Filing suit: context

Appendix B

Survey Instrument

1) Policy Domain:
    1. Transportation
    3. Education
    5. Civil rights

Background
  2a) This organization could best be described as a
    1. Profit-seeking firm
    5. Voluntary organization
  2b) [If a profit-seeking firm] Would you classify your organization as a
    1. Producer
    2. Distributor
    3. Retailer
    4. Service provider
    5. Other firm (How would you label it?)
  2c) [If a voluntary organization] Would you classify your organization as a
    1. Professional association
    2. Trade association
    3. Public interest group
    4. Research organization
    5. Trade union
    6. Other voluntary(How would you label it?)
    7. Association of governments
  3a) Is this the national headquarters of your organization or is your national headquarters elsewhere?
    1. National headquarters
    5. Located elsewhere (If elsewhere, where?)
    8. I do not know.
  3b) When did your organization first establish an office in Washington?

3c) When was the organization itself established?

4a) Generally speaking, how would describe your organization—
as liberal, middle-of-the-road, or conservative?
1. Liberal
3. Middle-of-the-road
5. Conservative
8. I do not know.

4b) Overall, is your organization closer to the Democratic Party, to
the Republican Party, or to neither party?
1. Democratic Party
3. Republican Party
5. Neither party
8. I do not know.

5a) In general, do the policy positions of this association tend to
call for:
MORE or LESS government regulation of business and industry?
More or MUCH more? Less or MUCH Less?

5b) In general, do the policy positions of this association tend to
call for:
MORE or LESS government provision of social services?
More or MUCH more? Less or MUCH Less?

6a) Many organizations are involved in a number of different policy areas. Here is a list of issues. Could you tell me which of
these policy areas your organization is particularly active in?
[Identify as many as appropriate]
1. Agriculture
2. Civil rights
3. Consumer rights
4. Defense
5. Domestic economic policy
6. Education
7. Energy
8. Environmental policy
9. Foreign policy
10. Health
11. Housing
12. International trade
13. Labor policy
14. Law enforcement
15. Social welfare/Social Security
16. Transportation
17. Urban development

Are there any other national policy areas in which your organization is active? If so, which?

6b) Of all of these categories, which *one* issue area is your organization most concerned with?

1. Agriculture
2. Civil rights
3. Consumer rights
4. Defense
5. Domestic economic policy
6. Education
7. Energy
8. Environmental policy
9. Foreign policy
10. Health
11. Housing
12. International trade
13. Labor policy
14. Law enforcement
15. Social welfare/Social Security
16. Transportation
17. Urban development
20. OTHER? (Specify.)

7) When you consider all of the policy areas listed above, what percentage of the total effort do you think you spend specifically on transportation [education/civil rights] issues?

Association Resources [If corporation, skip to corporate resources.]

8a) Does your organization have individual members?
1. Yes
5. No

8b) How many individual members do you have?

8c) Who joins?

9a) Do you have organizations/corporations/associations as members?
1. Yes
5. No [If no, skip to . . .]

9b) How many organizational members do you have?

9c) What kinds of organizations join?

10a) How many full-time-equivalent paid staff members does your organization have?

10b) How many of these work in governmental relations (full-time-equivalent)?

11a) Do you have volunteer staff members as well?
    1. Yes
    5. No
    8. I do not know
11b) [If yes] How many volunteers do you have on staff?
11c) [If yes] How many full-time equivalents would this be?
11d) [If yes] How many of these work in governmental relations?

Corporate Resources [Associations skip down to PAC section.]
12a) How many persons does your organization employ?
12b) How many staff members do you have working in governmental relations?

PACs (For All Organizations)
  13) Do you have an affiliated PAC?
    1. Yes (Could you tell me its name?)
    5. No
  14) Associations [excluding its political action committee]: What is the approximate annual budget of your organization?
    or
    Corporations [excluding its political action committee]: Approximately how much does your corporation budget annually for its government affairs operation?

Contact with Other Groups
15a) Does your organization have a board of directors?
    1. Yes
    5. No [You can skip to Expertise.]
15b) How many members are there?
16a) Do any members of your board of directors serve on the boards of other organizations?
    1. Yes
    5. No [Skip to Expertise.]
    8. I do not know
16b) [If yes] Can you identify any of these other organizations?
    1. Yes [Record names.]
    5. No
    8. I do not know
17a) Do you think that there are any advantages for your organization in having members on its board of directors who serve simultaneously on the boards of other organizations?
    1. Yes
    5. No

17b) [If yes] Would you say it is
    1. Very beneficial
    2. Somewhat beneficial

17c) [If yes] What are some of those advantages?

17d) Do members of the board serve as a path of communication and/or information to and from other organizations on whose boards they serve?
    1. Yes
    5. No
    8. I do not know.

17e) [If yes] How?

Expertise

I'm interested in how organizations build up expertise, and one way is by employing individuals who have worked for other organizations or the government.

18a) Thinking specifically about organizational leaders and those who work in governmental relations, how many of these staff members have experience working for the federal government?

18b) How many of these have worked for other organizations similar to yours—or have previous experience in this policy field?

18c) How useful for your organization are the contacts staff members have with organizations that they used to work for?
    1. Very useful
    2. Fairly useful
    3. Not that useful
    4. Not useful at all

Contact with Former Staff Members

19) I'd like you to think for a moment about any individuals who have left your government relations staff over the last couple years. Did any of them take positions at other organizations that are active in the transportation [education / civil rights] field?
    1. Yes
    5. No
    8. I do not know.

20) How important in general are relationships with former staff members in coordinating political action between this and other organizations? Are they:
    1. Very important
    2. Important
    3. Somewhat important
    4. Irrelevant

21) You do not need to identify individuals or organizations, but can you in your own mind think of a case where a *former* staff member is an important communications link to another organization?
    1. Yes
    5. No

Current Staff Contacts
22) Now, thinking of organizational leaders and the people who are currently working in governmental relations *at your organization*, off the top of your head, can you remember any groups or companies from which employees have come to work for your organization?
23) We have staff members who used to work for: (list)
24) How important are these staff members as a communications link to the organization they used to work for?
    1. Very important
    2. Important
    3. Somewhat important
    4. Not important
25a) Does your organization employ outside representatives or lobbyists?
    1. Yes
    5. No
    8. I do not know.
25b) [If yes] What's the name of the organization or individual that you retain or use most extensively?
25c) [If yes] Do these representatives represent other organizations on civil rights policy issues?
    1. Yes
    5. No
    8. I do not know.
25d) [If yes] Could you name any of these organizations?
    1. Yes (List below.)
    5. No
    8. I do not know.
26a) Does your organization employ outside attorneys or legal counsel?
    1. Yes
    5. No
    8. I do not know.
26b) [If yes] Do these attorneys represent other organizations in the civil rights field?

    1. Yes
    5. No
    8. I do not know.
26c) [If yes] Could you name any of these organizations?
    1. Yes (List below.)
    5. No
    8. I do not know.

Opinions on Coalition Strategies
I'm interested in knowing your opinions about the effectiveness of working together with other groups. Here are several related statements, and I'd like you to tell me how much you agree or disagree with them. For each statement, please tell me whether you:
    1. Agree strongly
    2. Agree somewhat
    3. Neither agree nor disagree
    4. Disagree somewhat, or
    5. Disagree strongly
27a) Short-term coalitions are easy to form.
    1 2 3 4 5
27b) Short-term coalitions are easy to maintain.
    1 2 3 4 5
27c) Long-term coalitions are easy to form.
    1 2 3 4 5
27d) Long-term coalitions are easy to maintain.
    1 2 3 4 5
27e) Being a member of a coalition helps an organization to control the outcome of an issue.
    1 2 3 4 5
27f) Coalitions are the way to be effective in politics.
    1 2 3 4 5
27g) If our organization does not join a coalition, we may lose our ability to shape the outcome of the issue.
    1 2 3 4 5
27h) Our membership in a coalition makes a difference
    1 2 3 4 5
27i) Being part of a coalition means that a group must surrender some of its independence or autonomy.
    1 2 3 4 5

Activities
I have listed a number of different activities and strategies that organizations employ in an effort to inform and/or influence the government. For each activity, could you tell me how important this

activity is for your organization: very important, important, not too important, or is it something that you do not do at all?

28a) Holding strategy meetings with other groups or firms
   1. Very important
   3. Important
   5. Not too important
   7. Don't do it

28b) Holding informal information-sharing meetings with other organizations
   1. Very important
   3. Important
   5. Not too important
   7. Don't do it

28c) Joining informal, onetime lobbying coalitions on specific pieces of legislation
   1. Very important
   3. Important
   5. Not too important
   7. Don't do it

28d) Joining informal lobbying coalitions that tend to re-form on several issues
   1. Very important
   3. Important
   5. Not too important
   7. Don't do it

28e) Belonging to a long-term, organized coalition of groups with a common interest
   1. Very important
   3. Important
   5. Not too important
   7. Don't do it

Cooperation with Other Organizations
I'd like to go over twelve more activities quickly, and in addition to asking you about how important these things are, I'd like to ask you the degree to which you do these things independently or in coordination with other organizations. For each activity, please tell me which option best describes how your organization conducts each task.
   1. We generally do this alone and independently from other groups.
   2. Although we generally act alone, we generally consult friendly groups.

3. We frequently coordinate this action with other groups whom we see as temporary coalition partners.
4. We frequently do this in close coordination with other groups whom we see as long-term coalition partners.
5. We do not do this action at all.

29a) Testifying at congressional hearings
1. Very important
3. Important
5. Not too important
7. Don't do it

29b) Context:
1. Alone and independently.
2. Alone, but consult friends.
3. In consultation with temporary coalition partners.
4. Close consultation with long-term coalition partners.
5. We do not do this

30a) Helping to draft legislation
1. Very important
3. Important
5. Not too important
7. Don't do it

30b) Context:
1. Alone and independently.
2. Alone, but consult friends.
3. In consultation with temporary coalition partners.
4. Close consultation with long-term coalition partners.
5. We do not do this.

31a) Helping to draft regulations, rules, or guidelines
1. Very important
3. Important
5. Not too important
7. Don't do it

31b) Context:
1. Alone and independently.
2. Alone, but consult friends.
3. In consultation with temporary coalition partners.
4. Close consultation with long-term coalition partners.
5. We do not do this.

32a) Alerting congressmen to the effects of a bill on their district
1. Very important
3. Important
5. Not too important
7. Don't do it

32b) Context:
   1. Alone and independently.
   2. Alone, but consult friends.
   3. In consultation with temporary coalition partners.
   4. Close consultation with long-term coalition partners.
   5. We do not do this.
33a) Making public endorsements of candidates for office
   1. Very important
   3. Important
   5. Not too important
   7. Don't do it
33b) Context:
   1. Alone and independently.
   2. Alone, but consult friends.
   3. In consultation with temporary coalition partners.
   4. Close consultation with long-term coalition partners.
   5. We do not do this.
34a) Publicizing candidates' voting records
   1. Very important
   3. Important
   5. Not too important
   7. Don't do it
34b) Context:
   1. Alone and independently.
   2. Alone, but consult friends.
   3. In consultation with temporary coalition partners.
   4. Close consultation with long-term coalition partners.
   5. We do not do this.
35a) Attempting to influence appointments to public office
   1. Very important
   3. Important
   5. Not too important
   7. Don't do it
35b) Context:
   1. Alone and independently.
   2. Alone, but consult friends.
   3. In consultation with temporary coalition partners.
   4. Close consultation with long-term coalition partners.
   5. We do not do this.
36a) Contributing work or personnel to electoral campaigns
   1. Very important
   3. Important
   5. Not too important
   7. Don't do it

36b) Context:
1. Alone and independently.
2. Alone, but consult friends.
3. In consultation with temporary coalition partners.
4. Close consultation with long-term coalition partners.
5. We do not do this.

37a) Making financial contributions to electoral campaigns through a PAC
1. Very important
3. Important
5. Not too important
7. Don't do it

37b) Context:
1. Alone and independently.
2. Alone, but consult friends.
3. In consultation with temporary coalition partners.
4. Close consultation with long-term coalition partners.
5. We do not do this.

38a) Generating grassroots mail to influence elected officials
1. Very important
3. Important
5. Not too important
7. Don't do it

38b) Context:
1. Alone and independently.
2. Alone, but consult friends.
3. In consultation with temporary coalition partners.
4. Close consultation with long-term coalition partners.
5. We do not do this.

39a) Contacting government officials directly to present your point of view
1. Very important
3. Important
5. Not too important
7. Don't do it

39b) Context:
1. Alone and independently.
2. Alone, but consult friends.
3. In consultation with temporary coalition partners.
4. Close consultation with long-term coalition partners.
5. We do not do this.

40a) Filing suit or otherwise engaging in litigation
1. Very important

3. Important
5. Not too important
7. Don't do it

40b) Context:

1. Alone and independently.
2. Alone, but consult friends.
3. In consultation with temporary coalition partners.
4. Close consultation with long-term coalition partners.
5. We do not do this.

Notes

CHAPTER 1

1. The event and its background are reported in Thomas W. Lippman, "Threatened Ban on Key Import Has Lobbyists Lining Up Behind Sudan Trade," *Washington Post*, 16 October 1997, sec. A, p. 6.

2. Saundra Torry, "Fearing Gain for Trial Lawyers, Business Groups Fight Tobacco Bill Harder," *Washington Post*, 19 May 1998, sec. A, p. 5.

3. Don Phillips, "Aviation Group to Push Safety Agenda: Coalition Wants Resources Used in Areas That Would Save the Most Lives," *Washington Post*, 12 February 1998, sec. A, p. 11.

4. Gamson's classic definition of a coalition as "the joint use of resources to determine the outcome of a mixed-motive situation involving more than two units" describes one type of coalition, but the definition is much too narrow to describe much of the coalition work among organized interests in Washington today. See William Gamson, "Experimental Studies of Coalition Formation," in *Advances in Experimental Social Psychology*, ed. Leonard Berkowitz (New York: Academic Press, 1964), 1:85. See also Barbara Hinckley, *Coalition Politics* (New York: Harcourt Brace Jovanovich, 1981), for a discussion of coalitions behavior across a wide range of political actors.

5. Ronald G. Shaiko, "Lobbying in Washington: A Contemporary Perspective," in *The Interest Group Connection: Electioneering, Lobbying, and Policymaking in Washington*, ed. Paul S. Herrnson, Ronald G. Shaiko, and Clyde Wilcox (Chatham, N.J.: Chatham House Publishers, 1998), 7.

6. Jeffrey M. Berry, *Lobbying for the People* (Princeton, N.J.: Princeton University Press, 1977); Jack L. Walker, "The Origins and Maintenance of Interest Groups in America," *American Political Science Review* 77 (June 1983): 390–406.

7. Thomas E. Mann, *A Question of Balance: The President, the Congress, and Foreign Policy* (Washington, D.C.: Brookings Institution, 1990), 14; Kay Lehman Schlozman and John T. Tierney, *Organized Interests and American Democracy* (New York: Harper and Row, 1986).

8. The number of corporations with a full-time Washington office has risen from 175 in 1968 to over 600 today. Shaiko, "Lobbying in Washington," 6.

9. Samuel Huntington, "The Democratic Distemper," *Public Interest* 10 (fall 1975): 9–38; Hugh Heclo, "Issue Networks and the Executive Establishment," in *The New American Political System*, ed. Anthony King (Washington, D.C.: American Enterprise Institute, 1978); Daniel McCool, "Subgovernments and the Impact of Policy Fragmentation and Accommodation," *Policy Studies*

Review 8 (1989): 264–87; Robert H. Salisbury, "The Paradox of Interest Groups in Washington—More Groups, Less Clout," in *The New American Political System*, 2d ed., ed. Anthony King (Washington, D.C.: American Enterprise Institute, 1990); James Q. Wilson, "American Politics, Then and Now," *Commentary* (February 1979): 39–46; Anthony King, "The American Polity in the Late 1970s: Building Coalitions in the Sand," in King, *The New American Political System* (1978).

10. Schlozman and Tierney, *Organized Interests*, 279.

11. Heclo, "Issue Networks," 88.

12. Thomas L. Gais, Mark A. Peterson, and Jack L. Walker, "Interest Groups, Iron Triangles and Representative Institutions in American National Government," *British Journal of Political Science* 14 (April 1984): 161–85. The most important works exploring the issue network concept include John P. Heinz, Edward O. Laumann, Robert L. Nelson, and Robert H. Salisbury, *The Hollow Core: Private Interests in National Policy Making* (Cambridge, Mass.: Harvard University Press, 1993); Christopher J. Bosso, *Pesticides and Politics: The Life Cycle of a Public Issue* (Pittsburgh: University of Pittsburgh Press, 1987); Jeffrey M. Berry, "Subgovernments, Issue Networks, and Political Conflict," in *Remaking American Politics*, ed. Richard A. Harris and Sidney M. Milkis (Boulder, Colo.: Westview Press, 1989), 239–60; and Jeffrey M. Berry, "The Dynamic Qualities of Issue Networks" (paper presented at the annual meeting of the American Political Science Association, New York, 1–4 September 1994).

13. Heclo, "Issue Networks," 104.

14. Ibid.

15. Ibid., 102.

16. Salisbury, "The Paradox of Interest Groups," 213.

17. Heinz, Laumann, Nelson, and Salisbury, *The Hollow Core*, 301.

18. Frank Swoboda, "Usually Squabbling Airlines Unite to Back a Travel Tax Plan," *Washington Post*, 10 July 1997, sec. E, p. 2.

19. Schlozman and Tierney, *Organized Interests*, 283–88; Robert H. Salisbury, John P. Heinz, Edward O. Laumann, and Robert L. Nelson, "Who Works with Whom? Interest Group Alliances and Opposition," *American Political Science Review* 81 (1987): 1217–34.

20. Burdett A. Loomis, "Coalitions of Interests: Building Bridges in the Balkanized State," in *Interest Group Politics*, 2d ed., ed. Allan J. Cigler and Burdett A. Loomis (Washington, D.C.: Congressional Quarterly Press, 1986), 258–74.

21. Virginia Gray and David Lowery, "To Lobby Alone or in a Flock: Foraging Behavior among Organized Interests," *American Politics Quarterly* 26, no. 1 (January 1998): 5–34.

22. The term "predigested policies" was coined by Douglas W. Costain and Anne N. Costain, in "Interest Groups as Policy Aggregators in the Legislative Process," *Polity* 14 (1981): 249–72. See also Schlozman and Tierney, *Organized Interests*, 307; and Bosso, *Pesticides and Politics*, 233.

23. Very briefly, Olson's central argument is that it is generally irrational to join a large group in pursuit of collective goods unless one receives selective benefits as well. See Mancur Olson, *The Logic of Collective Action* (Cambridge, Mass.: Harvard University Press, 1965).

24. Loomis uses the term "coalition brokers" to describe the role played by coalition founders. Loomis, "Coalitions of Interests," 270.

CHAPTER 2

1. See David J. Greenstone, "Group Theories," in *Handbook of Political Science*, vol. 4, ed. Fred I. Greenstein and Nelson W. Polsby (Reading, Mass.: Addison-Wesley, 1975); Robert H. Salisbury, "Interest Groups," in Greenstein and Polsby, *Handbook of Political Science*, vol. 4; David G. Garson, *Group Theories of Politics* (Beverly Hills, Calif.: Sage Publications, 1978); Allan J. Cigler, "Interest Groups: A Subfield in Search of an Identity," in *American Institutions*, vol. 4 of *Political Science: Looking to the Future*, ed. William Crotty (Evanston, Ill.: Northwestern University Press, 1991), pp. 99–135.

2. William P. Browne, *Private Interests, Public Policy, and American Agriculture* (Lawrence: University Press of Kansas, 1988), 1. The best known "broad theoretical treatments" are David Truman, *The Governmental Process* (New York: Alfred A. Knopf, 1951), and James Q. Wilson, *Political Organizations* (New York: Basic Books, 1973). Case studies abound, though Browne points to Andrew S. McFarland, *Common Cause: Lobbying in the Public Trust* (Chatham, N.J.: Chatham House, 1984), as archetypal. And, though Browne cites Lester W. Milbrath, *The Washington Lobbyists* (Chicago: Rand McNally and Company, 1963), as the long-standing empirical examination of note, better examples of more recent and more sophisticated empirical studies include Kay Lehman Schlozman and John T. Tierney's *Organized Interests and American Democracy* (New York: Harper and Row, 1986), and Jack L. Walker, Jr., *Mobilizing Interest Groups in America: Patrons, Professions, and Social Movements* (Ann Arbor: University of Michigan Press, 1991).

3. Browne, *Private Interests*, 1–3.

4. Henry J. Pratt, *The Gray Lobby* (Chicago: University of Chicago Press, 1976).

5. Loree Bykerk and Ardith Maney, "Consumer Groups and Coalition Politics on Capitol Hill," in *Interest Group Politics*, 4th ed., ed. Allan J. Cigler and Burdett A. Loomis (Washington D.C.: Congressional Quarterly Press, 1995).

6. Two notable examples of interviewing in a small number of specific policy domains for comparison are John P. Heinz, Edward O. Laumann, Robert L. Nelson, and Robert H. Salisbury, *The Hollow Core: Private Interests in National Policy Making* (Cambridge, Mass.: Harvard University Press, 1993), and Edward O. Laumann and David Knoke, *The Organizational State* (Madison: University of Wisconsin Press, 1987).

7. Douglas R. Arnold, "Overtilled and Undertilled Fields in American Politics," *Political Science Quarterly* 97 (spring 1982): 91–103.

8. Cigler, "Interest Groups: A Subfield in Search of an Identity," 100.

9. Jack L. Walker, Jr., "Activities and Maintenance Strategies of Interest Groups in the United States, 1980 and 1985" (Ann Arbor: University of Michigan, Institute of Public Policy Studies [producer], 1985; Ann Arbor: Interuniversity Consortium for Political and Social Research, [distributor], 1991), computer

file (ICPSR 9601); John P. Heinz, Edward O. Laumann, Robert L. Nelson, and Robert H. Salisbury, "Washington, DC, Representatives: Private Interests in National Policymaking, 1982–1983" (Chicago, Ill.: American Bar Foundation [producer], 1989; Ann Arbor: Interuniversity Consortium for Political and Social Research [distributor], 1995), Computer file (ICPSR 6040).

10. This is becoming even more the case with the cultural transformation caused by the computer. The Internet World Wide Web (WWW) sites for the United States Senate and the House of Representatives provide instantaneous access to full copies of the House and Senate Rules in their entirety and in summary form.

11. Cigler, "Interest Groups: A Subfield in Search of an Identity," 100.

12. Semour Dunbar, *A History of Travel in America* (New York: Tudor Publishing Co., 1937).

13. John R. Meyer, Merton J. Peck, John Stenason, and Charles Zwick, *The Economics of Competition in the Transportation Industries* (Cambridge, Mass.: Harvard University Press, 1959), 9; E. Grosvenor Plowman, "Influence of Transportation Users," in *Transportation Century*, ed. George Fox Mott (Baton Rouge: Louisiana State University Press, 1966), 29; Thomas J. DiLorenzo, "The Origins of Antitrust: An Interest-Group Perspective," *International Review of Law and Economics* 5 (1985): 73–90.

14. Charles L. Dearing and Wilfred Owen, *National Transportation Policy* (Washington, D.C.: Brookings Institution, 1949).

15. Diana Evans, "Reconciling Pork-Barrel Politics and National Transportation Policy: Highway Demonstration Projects," in *Who Makes Public Policy? The Struggle for Control between Congress and the Executive*, ed. Robert S. Gilmour and Alexis A. Halley (Chatham, N.J.: Chatham House, 1994), 42–61.

16. The introduction to Hulbert's analysis of transportation provides a gritty if enthusiastic reminder that the fierce competitiveness one finds in transportation is not a new phenomenon. Hulbert notes that there is "a rich fund of material in the perpetual rivalries of pack-horseman and wagoner, of riverman and canal boatman, of steamboat promoter and railway capitalist . . . at every point the old jostling and challenging the new: pack-horsemen demolishing wagons in the early days of the Alleghany [sic] traffic; wagoners deriding Clinton's Ditch; angry boatmen anxious to ram the paddle wheels of Fulton's *Clermont*, which threatened their monopoly." Archer B. Hulbert, *The Paths of Inland Commerce*, Chronicles of America Series, vol. 21 (New Haven: Yale University Press, 1920), vii.

17. Martha Derthick and Paul J. Quirk, *The Politics of Deregulation* (Washington, D.C.: Brookings Institution, 1985), 147–74.

18. National Advisory Committee on Education, *Federal Relations to Education, Report of The National Advisory Committee on Education*, Part 1, *Committee Findings and Recommendations* (Washington, D.C.: National Capital Press, 1931), 11.

19. Gordon Canfield Lee, *The Struggle for Federal Aid, First Phase: A History of the Attempts to Obtain Federal Aid for the Common Schools, 1870–1890* (New York: Teachers College, Columbia University, 1949), 17.

20. Educational Policies Commission, *Public Education and the Future of America* (Washington, D.C.: National Education Association, 1955), 32.

21. The "Big Six" for higher education are (alphabetically listed) the American Association of Community College (AACC), and the American Association of State Colleges and Universities (AASCU), the American Council on Education (ACE), the Association of American Universities (AAU), the National Association of Independent Colleges and Universities (NAICU), and the National Association of State Universities and Land-Grant Colleges (NASULGC).

22. Rene Sanchez, "Edison Project to Double Number of Schools," *Washington Post*, 27 May 1998, sec. A, p. 6.

23. Gunnar Myrdal, *An American Dilemma: The Negro Problem in Modern Democracy* (New York: Harper, 1944).

24. Doug McAdam, *Political Process and the Development of Black Insurgency, 1930–1970* (Chicago: University of Chicago Press, 1982), 71–72.

25. David Stannard, *The American Holocaust: Columbus and the Conquest of the New World* (London: Oxford University Press, 1992).

26. James H. Mundy, *Hard Times, Hard Men: Maine and the Irish, 1830–1860* (Scarborough, Maine: Harp Publications, 1990).

27. Don H. Tolzmann, ed., *German-Americans in the World Wars*, vol. 1, *The Anti-German Hysteria of World War One*, ed., Franziska Ott (Munich; New Providence, N.J.: K. G. Saur, 1995).

28. Leslie T. Hatamiya, *Righting a Wrong: Japanese Americans and the Passage of the Civil Liberties Act of 1988* (Stanford: Stanford University Press, 1993).

29. See John D'Emilio, *Sexual Politics, Sexual Communities: The Making of a Homosexual Minority in the United States, 1940–1970* (Chicago: University of Chicago Press, 1983).

30. Richard K. Scotch, *From Good Will to Civil Rights: Transforming Federal Disability Policy* (Philadelphia: Temple University Press, 1984); Stephen L. Percy, *Disability, Civil Rights, and Public Policy* (Tuscaloosa: University of Alabama Press, 1989).

31. Charles S. Bullock III and Charles M. Lamb, *Implementation of Civil Rights Policy* (Monterey, Calif.: Brooks/Cole Publishing Co., 1984).

32. See McAdam, *Political Process*; Jeffrey M. Berry, *The Interest Group Society*, 3d ed. (New York: Longman, 1997), 128–29. Indeed, many of the best-known demonstrations linked to the transportation and education domains were actually civil rights issues—e.g., the bus boycott and demonstrations over school desegregation and integration.

33. Schlozman and Tierney, *Organized Interests*, 149.

34. Graham Kalton, *Introduction to Survey Sampling*, Quantitative Applications in the Social Sciences Series, no. 35 (Newbury Park, Calif.: Sage Publications, 1983), 24–26.

35. I used the CIS index to look up transportation and transportation-related index entries, viz., air-, auto-, aviation-, freight, high speed ground transportation, inland water transportation, motor bus, motor transportation, passenger ship, rail-, rural transportation, ship-, transportation-, trucking. In addition to all hearings indexed under these topics, I examined all hearings conducted by the House Public Works and Transportation Committee, the Senate Commerce, Science, and Transportation Committee, and all subcommittees of those two bodies, whether the hearing was noted under the indexing terms or not.

36. The specific education-related hearings topics were adult education and literacy, bilingual education, business education, colleges and universities, community colleges, compensatory education, education, education regulation, educational _____, elementary and secondary education, federal aid to education, federal aid to higher education, federal aid to local governments: education, federal aid to vocational education, Headstart project, health education, illiteracy, preschool education, private schools, public schools, scholarships, school _____, special education, teaching aids and devices, technical education, vocational education and training. In addition to all hearings indexed under these topics, I examined all hearings conducted by the House Education and Labor Committee, the Senate Labor and Human Resources Committee, or their respective subcommittees.

37. The specific index headings for civil rights were age discrimination, civil rights, Civil Rights Act, Civil Rights Attorney's Fees Act, Civil Rights Division (Justice Department), Commission on Civil Rights, Civil Rights of Institutionalized Persons Act, discrimination against the handicapped, discrimination in education, discrimination in employment, discrimination in housing, homosexual rights, racial discrimination, and women's rights. In addition to all hearings indexed under these topics, I examined all hearings conducted by the House and Senate Judiciary Committees and their subcommittees.

38. The difference in size comes primarily from the narrowness and diversity of the legislative agendas in the 101st Congress. The biggest single civil rights bill before the 101st Congress was the Americans with Disabilities Act of 1990.

39. The table used can be found in John E. Freund, *Mathematical Statistics*, 2d ed. (Englewood Cliffs, N.J.: Prentice-Hall, Inc., 1971), 444ff.

40. Arthur C. Close, ed., *Washington Representatives 1990*, 14th ed. (Washington, D.C.: Columbia Books, 1990), was the most important directory utilized. On some occasions, a respondent would volunteer unprompted, off-the-cuff recommendations about another group—e.g., "You know, you really should talk to John Doe at the ABC group." In cases where the "ABC group" was actually in the sample and had yet to be contacted, that recommendation was taken under advisement, though to preserve the privacy and anonymity of the sample I never indicated to respondents whether or not I would in fact contact a specific organization at all.

41. Lewis Anthony Dexter, *Elite and Specialized Interviewing* (Evanston, Ill.: Northwestern University Press, 1970); Don A. Dillman, *Mail and Telephone Surveys: The Total Design Method* (New York: John Wiley and Sons, 1978), 39–78.

42. Though the use of the phone prevented me from using "show cards" to display lists of issues and possible response categories for the respondents, the lack of show cards proved not to be an onerous challenge. Show cards allow the respondent to see questions or options as well as hearing them verbally. This is particularly helpful when survey instruments deal with lists, such as the list of political and policy activities in this project. See Jean M. Converse and Stanley Presser, *Survey Questions: Handcrafting the Standardized Questionnaire*, Quantitative Applications in the Social Sciences Series, no. 63 (Newbury Park, Calif.: Sage Publications, 1986), 14.

43. Herbert F. Weisberg, Jon A. Krosnick, and Bruce D. Bowen, *An Introduction to Survey Research and Data Analysis*, 2d ed. (Glenview, Ill.: Scott, Foresman and Co., 1989), 100–101.

44. Ibid., 87.

45. This particular category consisted of two items requesting data on how many long-term coalitions the organization participated in and the approximate membership of each. The two items were discarded from the survey instrument very early in the interviewing process. It became apparent after several interviews that the questions were very difficult for respondents to answer, and the information provided was of questionable accuracy at best. In many cases, respondents were unaware of the coalitions that colleagues were attending. The most frequent responses were "I have no idea," "I don't know what the others are doing," and "I'd have to make a list, and I don't have that kind of time."

46. In addition to gathering new data on previously unexplored topics, the survey instrument was constructed to allow me to replicate and flesh out specific data collected in earlier studies such as those reported in Schlozman and Tierney, *Organized Interests*, and Laumann and Knoke, *The Organizational State.*

CHAPTER 3

1. Quoted in Jeffrey H. Birnbaum, *The Lobbyists: How Influence Peddlers Get Their Way in Washington* (New York: Times Books, 1992), 84.

2. This definition distinguishes purposive coalitions which coordinate and undertake joint political action from the myriad of other groups which function solely as information clearinghouses or social gatherings for Washington organizational representatives. This definition is not, however, intended to exclude the political coalitions that may spin off of these other groups of organizations.

3. Mancur Olson, *The Logic of Collective Action* (Cambridge, Mass.: Harvard University Press, 1965); Robert H. Salisbury, "An Exchange Theory of Interest Groups," *Midwest Journal of Political Science* 13 (February 1969): 1–32.

4. Clark and Wilson use the term "purposive" rather than expressive. Peter B. Clark and James Q. Wilson, "Incentive Systems: A Theory of Organizations," *Administrative Science Quarterly* 6 (September 1961): 219–66. Salisbury develops the concept of expressive benefits in "An Exchange Theory of Interest Groups."

5. Wilson notes briefly that Olson's logic "may be more applicable to coalitions of organizations than to those of individuals" because individuals "will often contribute to large organizations without receiving any specific, material benefit from it; organizations rarely will." I disagree with this in the context of political coalitions. As I will argue below, symbolic benefits are often exchanged for symbolic contributions. Though Wilson notes examples of coalitions and general theories of coalition building, he surprisingly does not develop this theme in the framework of entrepreneurship or exchange theory one might have expected. James Q. Wilson, *Political Organizations* (New York: Basic Books, 1973). The quotation is from page 277.

6. Indeed, for this reason much of the discussion of legislative coalitions which focuses upon the "minimum winning coalition" does not apply to the real-world decisions made by Washington organizational representatives. As Berry points out, "Operationally, there is no such thing as a minimum winning coalition for public interest groups. They will always be trying to expand membership so as to increase what they consider to be inferior resources." This point need not be limited to public interest groups. Jeffrey M. Berry, *Lobbying for the People* (Princeton, N.J.: Princeton University Press, 1977), 259 n. 4. On the implications of reducing Olson's assumption of perfect information, see Terry Moe, *The Organization of Interests* (Chicago: University of Chicago Press, 1980).

7. Samuel Huntington, "The Democratic Distemper," *Public Interest* 10 (fall 1975): 9–38; Hugh Heclo, "Issue Networks and the Executive Establishment," in *The New American Political System*, ed. Anthony King (Washington, D.C.: American Enterprise Institute, 1978); Daniel McCool, "Subgovernments and the Impact of Policy Fragmentation and Accommodation," *Policy Studies Review* 8 (winter 1989): 264–87.

8. Burdett A. Loomis, "Coalitions of Interests: Building Bridges in the Balkanized State," in *Interest Group Politics*, 2d ed., ed. Allan J. Cigler and Burdett A. Loomis (Washington, D.C.: Congressional Quarterly Press, 1986); William P. Browne, *Private Interests, Public Policy, and American Agriculture* (Lawrence: University Press of Kansas, 1988).

9. Jeffrey M. Berry, "Subgovernments, Issue Networks, and Political Conflict," in *Remaking American Politics*, ed. Richard A. Harris and Sidney M. Milkis (Boulder: Westview Press, 1989), 236–60.

10. Steven S. Smith and Christopher J. Deering, *Committees in Congress*, 2d ed. (Washington, D.C.: Congressional Quarterly Press, 1990).

11. Christopher J. Bosso, *Pesticides and Politics: The Life Cycle of a Public Issue* (Pittsburgh: University of Pittsburgh Press, 1987), 249.

12. Steven R. Weisman, "No. 1, the President Is Very Result Oriented," *New York Times*, 12 November 1983, 10, quoted in Samuel Kernell, *Going Public: New Strategies of Presidential Leadership*, 2d ed. (Washington, D.C.: Congressional Quarterly Press, 1993), 30.

13. Jeffrey M. Berry, *The Interest Group Society*, 2d ed. (Glenview, Ill.: Scott, Foresman and Co., 1989), 165.

14. Berry, *Lobbying for the People*; Jack L. Walker, "The Origins and Maintenance of Interest Groups in America," *American Political Science Review* 77 (June 1983): 390–406; Kay Lehman Schlozman and John T. Tierney, *Organized Interests and American Democracy* (New York: Harper and Row, 1986); Thomas E. Mann, *A Question of Balance: The President, the Congress, and Foreign Policy* (Washington, D.C.: Brookings Institution, 1990), 14.

15. E. Pendleton Herring, *Group Representation before Congress* (Baltimore: Johns Hopkins Press, 1929), 19.

16. Ronald G. Shaiko, "Lobbying in Washington: A Contemporary Perspective," in *The Interest Group Connection: Electioneering, Lobbying, and Policymaking in Washington* (Chatham, N.J.: Chatham House, 1998), 7.

17. Herring, *Group Representation*, 46.

18. Heclo, "Issue Networks," 96.

19. Robert H. Salisbury, "The Paradox of Interest Groups in Washington— More Groups, Less Clout," in *The New American Political System*, 2d ed., ed. Anthony King (Washington, D.C.: American Enterprise Institute, 1990).

20. Jonathan Rauch, *Demosclerosis: The Silent Killer of American Government* (New York: Times Books, 1994). Wright provides a balanced assessment of the relationship between interest groups and policy gridlock in John R. Wright, *Interest Groups and Congress: Lobbying, Contributions, and Influence* (Boston: Allyn and Bacon: 1996), 166–81.

21. Raymond A. Bauer, Ithiel de Sola Pool, and Lewis Anthony Dexter, *American Business and Public Policy: The Politics of Foreign Trade*, 2d ed. (New York: Aldine Publishing Co., 1972), 414.

22. Douglas W. Costain and Anne N. Costain, "Interest Groups as Policy Aggregators in the Legislative Process," *Polity* 14, no. 2 (winter 1981): 249–72. Also see the briefer treatment in Kay Lehman Schlozman and John T. Tierney, *Organized Interests*, 307; and Christopher Bosso, *Pesticides and Politics*, 233.

23. Rep. John D. Dingell (D-MI) was actually *chairman* of the House Committee on Energy and Commerce at the time.

24. James Q. Wilson, *Political Organizations* (New York: Basic Books, 1973; reprint, Princeton, N.J.: Princeton University Press, 1995), 317 (page citation is to the reprint edition).

25. Rep. William Ford (D-MI) was chairman of the House Committee on Education and Labor, as well as chairman of the Subcommittee on Postsecondary Education and Training.

26. John Schwartz, "Unlikely Allies Opposed Anti-Smoking Campaign," *Washington Post*, 20 January 1998, sec. A, p. 3.

27. In the extreme comparative case, absence from that kind of coalition could leave a small group in a position similar to that of organized interests in corporatist societies that are not recognized by the state as representative groups and are therefore excluded from negotiations. For a brief review of the literature on interest groups and corporatism, see Ruth Berins Collier and David Collier, "Inducements versus Constraints: Disaggregating 'Corporatism,'" *American Political Science Review* 73 (1979): 967–86; and Leo Panitch, "Recent Theorizations of Corporatism: Reflections on a Growth Industry," *British Journal of Sociology* 31 (1980): 159–87.

28. Charls E. Walker, "A Four-Decade Perspective on Lobbying in Washington," in *The Interest Group Connection: Electioneering, Lobbying and Policymaking in Washington*, ed. Paul S. Herrnson, Ronald G. Shaiko, and Clyde Wilcox (Chatham, N.J.: Chatham House Publishers, 1998), 28.

29. The large number of "neither agree nor disagree" responses among education groups on question 3 is particularly high because of the number of groups who differentiated between appropriations and authorization in that policy domain. The modal response for this group ran along the lines of "I agree *and* disagree. For appropriations, it's very important for us to be in CEF, but for authorizations, we can act more on our own." It should be noted that CEF takes no positions on authorization issues.

30. This uniform belief in the efficacy of coalitions across all three policy spheres is underscored by a chi-square test, which shows no significant differences between the policy fields. The χ^2 value for the responses to the first

question, "Coalitions are the way to be effective in politics" was 4.81. The χ^2 value for the second question, "Being a member of a coalition helps an organization to control the outcome of an issue," was 6.25. The χ^2 value for the final efficacy statement, "If our organization does not join a coalition, we may lose our ability to shape the outcome of the issue," was 11.60. None of these values are significant with 8 degrees of freedom, even at the relaxed significance level of 0.1.

31. Robert H. Salisbury, John P. Heinz, Edward O. Laumann, and Robert L. Nelson, "Who Works With Whom? Interest Group Alliances and Opposition," *American Political Science Review* 81, no. 4 (December 1987): 1217–34; Edward O. Laumann and David Knoke, *The Organizational State* (Madison: University of Wisconsin Press, 1987); John P. Heinz, Edward O. Laumann, Robert H. Salisbury, and Robert L. Nelson, "Inner Circles or Hollow Cores? Elite Networks in National Policy Systems," *Journal of Politics* 52, no. 2 (May 1990): 356–90.

32. Jeffrey M. Berry, letter to author, 3 May 1995.

33. John W. Kingdon develops the window-of-opportunity concept in *Agendas, Alternatives, and Public Policies* (Boston: Little, Brown, 1984).

34. The principal-agent theory explains some organizational behaviors as the outgrowth of asymmetries in information between organizations (the principals) and their agents. In large organizations, agents have a broad latitude of discretion because of inadequate possibilities for supervision by the principal. Thus, agents have broad opportunities to "shirk" responsibilities. See Stephen A. Ross, "The Economic Theory of Agency: The Principal's Problem," *American Economic Review* 63, no. 2 (May 1973): 134–39; Joseph A. Stiglitz, "Risk Sharing and Incentives in Sharecropping," *Review of Economic Studies* 61 (April 1974): 219–56; Carl Shapiro and Joseph E. Stiglitz, "Equilibrium Unemployment as a Worker Discipline Device," *American Economic Review* 74, no. 3 (June 1984): 433–44; Glenn MacDonald, "New Directions in the Economic Theory of Agency," *Canadian Journal of Economics* 17 (August 1985): 415–40.

CHAPTER 4

1. Loomis introduces the term "coalition brokers" in Burdett A. Loomis, "Coalitions of Interests: Building Bridges in the Balkanized State," in *Interest Group Politics*, 2d ed., ed. Allan J. Cigler and Burdett A. Loomis (Washington, D.C.: Congressional Quarterly Press, 1986).

2. Jean-Jacques Rousseau, *The First and Second Discourses, Together with the Replies to Critics and Essay on the Origin of Languages*, ed., trans., and ann. Victor Gourevitch (New York: Harper and Row, 1986), 172–73 (pages 166–67 in the *Pleiade* standard pagination of Rousseau's *Oeuvres completes*.)

3. Kenneth N. Waltz, *Man, the State, and War: A Theoretical Analysis* (New York: Columbia University Press, 1959).

4. Robert H. Salisbury, John P. Heinz, Edward O. Laumann, and Robert L. Nelson, "Who Works with Whom? Interest Group Alliances and Opposition," *American Political Science Review* 81, no. 4 (December 1987): 1217–34.

5. John P. Heinz, Edward O. Laumann, Robert L. Nelson, and Robert H. Salisbury, *The Hollow Core: Private Interests in National Policy Making* (Cambridge, Mass.: Harvard University Press, 1993), 346.

6. Arturo Vargas, "Coalitions Once, Coalitions Again," *Hispanic* 8, no. 8 (September 1995): 88.

7. E. E. Schattschneider, *The Semisovereign People: A Realist's View of Democracy in America* (1960; reprint, Hinsdale, Ill.: Dryden Press, 1975).

CHAPTER 5

1. Robert H. Salisbury, "The Paradox of Interest Groups in Washington—More Groups, Less Clout," in *The New American Political System*, 2d ed., ed. Anthony King (Washington, D.C.: American Enterprise Institute, 1990), 204.

2. John W. Kingdon, *Agendas, Alternatives, and Public Policies* (Boston: Little, Brown, 1984). Kingdon argues that policy entrepreneurs seek to link pet projects to the problem *de jour*: "Advocates of a new policy initiative not only take advantage of politically propitious moments but also claim that their proposal is a solution to a pressing problem" (p. 211). The coupling of problem, policy, and politics is possible when a window of opportunity opens for the entrepreneur. Kingdon's garbage can model is adapted from the model presented in Michael Cohen, James March, and Johan Olsen, "A Garbage Can Model of Organizational Choice," *Administrative Science Quarterly* 17 (March 1972): 1–25.

3. The term "externality group" was introduced to the interest group literature in Don F. Hadwiger, *The Politics of Agricultural Research* (Lincoln: University of Nebraska Press, 1982).

4. Salisbury, "The Paradox of Interest Groups," 210.

5. Edward O. Laumann and David Knoke, *The Organizational State* (Madison: University of Wisconsin Press, 1987), 3.

6. The Americans with Disabilities Act (ADA) provides perhaps the most extensive recent examples of this externality group phenomenon. This "civil rights" legislation not only pulled in the predictable disability and business/employer organizations, but mobilized innumerable less obvious organizations representing architects, transit authorities, and gas station operators, to name a few.

7. See, e.g., Laumann and Knoke, *The Organizational State*, 194, and Howard E. Aldrich, *Organizations and Environments* (Englewood Cliffs, N.J.: Prentice-Hall, 1979).

8. E. E. Schattschneider, *The Semisovereign People* (1960; reprint, Hinsdale, Ill.: Dryden Press, 1975).

9. Charles S. Mack, *Lobbying and Government Relations: A Guide for Executives* (New York: Quorum Books, 1989), 119, citing Edward A. Grefe, "Creating Winning Coalitions," *Public Affairs Challenge* (fall 1983).

10. Ibid.

11. Laumann and Knoke, *The Organizational State*; John P. Heinz, Edward O. Laumann, Robert H. Salisbury, and Robert L. Nelson, "Inner Circles or Hollow Cores? Elite Networks in National Policy Systems," *Journal of Politics* 52 (1990): 356–90.

12. Hugh Heclo, *A Government of Strangers: Executive Politics in Washington* (Washington, D.C.: Brookings Institution, 1977).

13. Ibid., 111.

14. For several critical assessments of this school of thought, see G. Calvin MacKenzie, ed., *The In-and-Outers: Presidential Appointees and Transient Government in Washington* (Baltimore: Johns Hopkins University Press, 1987).

15. Hugh Heclo, "Issue Networks and the Executive Establishment," in *The New American Political System*, ed. Anthony King (Washington, D.C.: American Enterprise Institute, 1978), 108.

16. See Paul Quirk, *Industry Influence in Federal Regulatory Agencies* (Princeton, N.J.: Princeton University Press, 1981), especially chapter 5, and Jeffrey E. Cohen, "The Dynamics of the 'Revolving Door' on the FCC," *American Journal of Political Science* 30 (November 1986): 689–708, on the degree to which the potential for a future job with industry may impact the decisions of agency executives.

17. Dennis Thompson, *Ethics in Congress* (Washington, D.C.: Brookings Institution, 1995), 59. Similarly, concerns about conflict of interest during public service have led Congress to enact a substantial body of legislation requiring individuals entering public service from the private sector to "declare and divest" financial commitments that could fall under the scope of their regulation, and in several cases, to place their personal financial portfolios into blind trusts lest they face a conflict of interest. For a seminal analysis of these issues, see the Association of the Bar of the City of New York, Special Committee on the Federal Conflict of Interest Laws, *Conflict of Interest and Federal Service* (Cambridge, Mass.: Harvard University Press, 1960).

18. See especially Hugh Heclo, "The In-and-Outer System: A Critical Assessment," *Political Science Quarterly* 103 (spring 1988): 37–56.

19. Robert H. Salisbury and Paul Johnson, with John P. Heinz, Edward O. Laumann, and Robert L. Nelson, "Who You Know versus What You Know: The Uses of Government Experience for Washington Lobbyists," *American Journal of Political Science* 33 (1989): 175–95.

20. Heclo, *A Government of Strangers*, 102–3.

21. Cindy Skrzycki, "Lobbyist Is Top Choice to Head Chamber," *Washington Post*, 4 June 1997, sec. C, p. 13.

22. Ibid.

23. The interlock concept has been used since at least 1913, when the Pujo Committee used the concept to assess the role of financial institutions in the economy. As Mintz and Schwartz point out in a particularly helpful but succinct review of the literature, this along with other, nongovernmental research, contributed to the proscription of certain types of director interlocks in the Clayton Antitrust Act. Beth Mintz and Michael Schwartz, "Interlocking Directorates and Interest Group Formation," *American Sociological Review* 46 (December 1981): 851–69. For another early application of the concept, see Louis Brandeis, *Other People's Money* (New York: Frederick A. Stokes Co., 1914).

24. Maurice Zeitlin, "Corporate Ownership and Control: The Large Corporation and the Capitalist Class," *American Journal of Sociology* 79 (1974): 1073–1119; Beth Mintz and Michael Schwartz, *The Power Structure of American Business* (Chicago: University of Chicago Press, 1985); Michael Useem, *The Inner Circle* (New York: Oxford University Press, 1984); Mark S. Mizruchi, *The Structure of*

Corporate Political Action: Interfirm Relations and Their Consequences (Cambridge, Mass.: Harvard University Press, 1992).

25. Classic views of the power elite can be found in C. Wright Mills, *The Power Elite* (1956; reprint, London: Oxford University Press, 1974), and Useem, *The Inner Circle.*

26. A "don't know" response contains valuable information in itself. Since the immediate question of this chapter is how organizations overcome an information problem, this response means that they do not rely on board members for information about other organizations. The broader question being examined here is the degree to which governmental affairs representatives coordinate their activities with other organizations; here, a "don't know" response on board interlocks means that governmental affairs representatives do not attempt to coordinate action with other groups through the board of directors.

27. Specialization of attorneys among transportation groups is significant at the 0.1 level with chi-square (2 d.f.) of 3.12. Among education groups, specialization of attorneys is significant at the 0.025 level with chi-square (2 d.f.) of 6.12. A chi-square test is not appropriate for the civil rights data because the expected value for the two cells containing zeros would be less than one.

28. William L. Riordon, *Plunkitt of Tammany Hall* (New York: E. P. Dutton, 1963), 3.

CHAPTER 6

1. For an early foreshadowing of the nexus of politics and electronic communications, see Ithiel de Sola Pool, ed., *Talking Back: Citizen Feedback and Cable Technology* (Cambridge, Mass.: MIT Press, 1973), especially chapter 5, "Politics in a Wired Nation" by Pool and Herbert E. Alexander, 64–102. Michael E. Kraft and Norman J. Vig provide a particularly impressive collection of essays on the effects of technology and governmental attempts to direct its development in *Technology and Politics* (Durham, N.C.: Duke University Press, 1988). The potential challenges to democratic theory posed by technological development are approached with the tools of political philosophy in Richard B. Day, Ronald Beiner, and Joseph Masciulli, eds., *Democratic Theory and Technological Society* (Armonk, N.Y.: M. E. Sharpe, Inc., 1988).

2. Ithiel de Sola Pool, *Technologies of Freedom* (Cambridge, Mass.: Harvard University Press, 1983), 251.

3. Jeffrey M. Berry, *The Interest Group Society*, 2d ed. (Glenview, Ill.: Scott, Foresman, 1989), 58.

4. Several respondents noted this development in 1992 and 1993 interviews.

5. That is, at the time of the interview in the summer of 1993.

6. "57 Million Web Users Reported," *Editor and Publisher* 131, no. 19 (9 May 1998): 27. The study, conducted by RelevantKnowledgeInc, surveyed ten thousand individuals in fifty states using an equal-probability sample with random-digit-dialing.

7. Despite this speed, as Jeffrey M. Berry notes, the evolution of communication from phone calls and direct mail to faxes and Internet links represents variations on a theme rather than a new symphony. The new methods of communication and their corresponding speed do not change the basic dynamic of mobilization. Letter to the author, 29 March 1995 (appropriately enough, via e-mail).

8. <http://thomas.loc.gov>

9. Cynthia Morgan, "The Search Is On," *Windows Magazine*, November 1997, 214.

10. ".com sites explode," *Industry Week* (18 May 1998), 13.

11. Francisco Caceres, "The 'Click Here' Economy," *Business Week*, 22 June 1998, 122.

12. Now represented on over two hundred Web sites, for years the coalition originated at http://www.circus.com/~no_dhmo/. Even careful readers may be misled by the apparent legitimacy of this home page warning of the dangers of this chemical substance which surrounds us, causing hundreds of deaths each year through inhalation. The parody is revealed only if the interested reader reasons out the chemical composition of the dreaded dihydrogen monoxide: H_2O.

13. Bill McAllister, "Web Venture Links Lobby, Legislation," *Washington Post*, 27 January 1998, sec. A, p. 15.

14. Rajiv Chandrasekaran, "Ensuring Congress Gets the Word," *Washington Business*, 15 January 1998, 15.

15. Stanton McCandlish <mech@eff.org>, "Coalition Forms to oppose Exon 'decency' bill, S314/HR1004," [Usenet post], in <alt.activism, alt.activism.d, alt.censorship, alt.politics.datahighway, alt.wired, comp.org.cpsr.talk, comp.org.eff.news, comp.org.eff.talk>, 3 March 1995.

16. Though a typical newsgroup does not have millions of readers, it is a relatively simple, albeit unpopular, procedure to "spam" the Internet, generating a message on every one of the over ten thousand Usenet newsgroups in existence. This obviously defeats the advantage of being able to target only the self-selected interested parties subscribing to a relevant newsgroup, and it is likely to stimulate a vigorous response in the form of "flames" and "mailbombs" from disgruntled readers who find the message nongermane to their newsgroups. Spamming is not taken lightly in the self-policing cyber-community.

17. The generational effect is also obvious from survey data. A survey of Internet users done in 1994 by the Graphics, Visualization and Usability Center at Georgia Tech showed that 62 percent of respondents were under thirty years old, and only 5 percent were over fifty. Cited in Cheryl Currid, "Windows at Work," *Windows Magazine*, April 1995, 50. Gender effects are decreasing noticeably. Whereas only 5 percent of the Web users in the 1994 GVU survey noted above were female, approximately 40 percent of the 1997 GVU survey are female. See "GVU's 8th WWW User Survey," Online document available at <http://www.gvu.gatech.edu/user_surveys/survey-1997-10/>. Accessed 10 June 1998.

18. Though the composition of the Web is constantly changing, the growth

rate is instructive. As of 10 June 1998, Yahoo! listed 214 Republican Web Sites, 153 Democratic Web sites, and 243 sites for other parties, including 64 sites for libertarians. On 23 September 1996 there were only 44 Republican sites, 35 Democratic sites, and 32 Libertarian sites listed. Online Directory, available at <http://www.yahoo.com/Government/Politics/Parties/>.

19. John Pike <johnpike@fas.org>, "Re: CFR: Imperial Brain Trust for the New World Order!" [Usenet Post], in <alt.politics.org.cia>, 13 September 1995. As a simple example of how the Internet caters to diverse and otherwise marginalized groups, consider that this quote comes from a reply cross-posted to: <alt.conspiracy, alt.illuminati, alt.politics.usa.constitution, alt.activism, alt.politics.nationalism.white, alt.politics.radical-left, alt.politics.org.cfr, alt.politics.org.covert, alt.politics.org.cia, alt.politics.org.nsa, alt.politics.org.fbi, alt.politics.libertarian, talk.politics.libertarian, alt.individualism>.

20. Indeed, information which a few years ago would have been practically impossible to obtain is often readily available. A particularly surprising example is that of the American intelligence community. Students of intelligence can seek information from the Central Intelligence Agency directly on the CIA's WWW home-page <http://www.odci.gov/cia/>, or for a freer debate, can turn to the alt.politics.org.cia newsgroup. Not a day goes by without over a dozen posts to the newsgroup floating rumors overheard on the Washington subway, transcriptions of declassified data obtained through Freedom of Information Act requests, and referrals to other on-line sources of information about what American intelligence is up to domestically and abroad. The openness of this kind of monitoring no doubt has made more than one government official shudder.

21. Robert Wright, "Voice of America," *The New Republic,* 13 September 1993, 25.

22. This point was brought up by Susan Hula. Personal conversation, 12 February 1995.

23. Reading newsgroups without posting is a common practice, which has been given the rather dramatic name "lurking." On the other hand, many individuals choose to post anonymously to newsgroups by sending their messages through a remailer service that strips the automatic return address from a message before forwarding it on to the newsgroup.

CHAPTER 7

1. The clearest articulation of this principle is actually directed at the occupants of the Oval Office in chapter 4 of Richard Neustadt's classic *Presidential Power.* The most recent edition is *Presidential Power and the Modern Presidents: The Politics of Leadership from Roosevelt to Reagan* (New York: Free Press, 1990). However, as the text indicates, I am using the term "reputation" in a significantly narrower sense than Neustadt did.

2. The implications of this definition can be quickly derived. Groups without members, money, or expertise lack significance. Groups without name recognition or a message that differs from other established groups lack identity. Backstabbers, liars, and counterfeits lack legitimacy.

3. See William P. Browne, "Issue Niches and the Limits of Interest Group Influence," in *Interest Group Politics*, 3d ed., ed. Allan J. Cigler and Burdett A. Loomis (Washington, D.C.: Congressional Quarterly Press, 1991), 345–70, as well as his article "Organized Interests and Their Issue Niches: A Search for Pluralism in a Policy Domain," *Journal of Politics* 52 (1990): 477–509.

4. Jeffrey M. Berry, *The Interest Group Society* (Boston: Little, Brown, 1984), 202.

5. There is a somewhat Machiavellian concept present, just under the surface. One needs to develop a reputation independent of the particular policy battles that may come about because it is not clear that one will be able to enhance one's reputation in that battle where coalition partners may be necessary. The Prince might build up a reputation by a few extraordinary public acts in order to be able to wield his power as he desires on a day to day basis.

6. The public debate over specific interest group campaign contributions goes back at least to the House's 1854 Letcher Committee investigation and 1855 report chronicling the $10,000 payoff of a member of Congress by lobbyist Alexander Hay on behalf of gun manufacturer Samuel Colt. Aside from the cash involved, Hay passed out expensive revolvers to various politicians in order to secure the renewal of Colt's revolver patent. See Karl Schriftgiesser, *The Lobbyists: The Art and Business of Influencing Lawmakers* (Boston: Little, Brown, 1951), 10; James Deakin, *The Lobbyists* (Washington, D.C.: Public Affairs Press, 1966), 58; and Rep. Emanuel Celler, "Pressure Groups in Congress," *Annals* 319 (September 1958): 2–9.

7. Lester W. Milbrath, *The Washington Lobbyists* (Chicago: Rand McNally, 1963), 283. Milbrath traces the theme to Paul W. Cherington and Ralph L. Gillen's *The Business Representative in Washington* (Washington, D.C.: Brookings Institution, 1962), 57.

8. As Jacobson and Kernell note, "Contributions intended to curry favor are not made with an eye to electoral utility; the idea is to buy influence, not to affect the outcome. If an incumbent is certain to win, so much the better. This explains the behavioral law that much more of this money is available to incumbents certain to win than to challengers certain to lose. How much any particular incumbent collects depends largely on what he is prepared to solicit and accept." Gary C. Jacobson and Samuel Kernell, *Strategy and Choice in Congressional Elections* (New Haven: Yale University Press, 1981), 36. For the full evidence, Jacobson and Kernell refer the reader to Gary C. Jacobson, *Money in Congressional Elections* (New Haven: Yale University Press, 1980), 113–23.

9. Schlozman and Tierney point out that the often-drawn distinction between access and influence is "less clearly defined than it is sometimes assumed to be." Kay Lehman Schlozman and John T. Tierney, *Organized Interests and American Democracy* (New York: Harper and Row, 1986), 164.

10. David B. Truman, *The Governmental Process* (New York: Alfred A. Knopf, 1951), 339.

11. Heclo points out another important face of the self-differentiation incentive: "A key factor in the proliferation of groups is the almost inevitable tendency of successfully enacted policies unwittingly to propagate hybrid interests . . . . The point is that even when government is not pursuing a deliberate strategy of divide and conquer, its activist policies greatly increase the incentives for groups to form around the differential effects of these policies, each refusing to allow any other group to speak in its name." Hugh Heclo, "Issue Networks and the Executive Establishment," in *The New American Political System*, ed. Anthony King (Washington, D.C.: American Enterprise Institute, 1978), 96.

12. Ruth Marcus, "Business, Lobbying Firms Primed for 'Super Bowl of Schmooze,'" *Washington Post*, 12 August 1996, sec. A, p. 15.

13. Ibid.

14. This is similar to Richard F. Fenno's concepts of "member goals" and "strategic premises" in *Congressmen in Committees* (Boston: Little, Brown, 1973). However, where Fenno is concerned with the strategic premises leading to decision rules in committees that members join because of their goals, the "enabling strategies" which I address are those early strategies that group leaders employ in order to best position themselves for later phases of the policy process.

15. This view is presented by Julius Cohen, "Hearing on a Bill: Legislative Folklore?" *Minnesota Law Review* 37 (1952): 38–39. Though Schlozman and Tierney do not seem to hold the view that testimony is more show than policy vehicle, they do note the attention given by groups to the presence of TV cameras, the practice of supplying questions to friendly committee members, and the practice of the legislators and committee staff to stack the deck by bringing in particularly strong witnesses in favor of their position and minimizing opposition testimony, as well as treating friendly and opposition witnesses to very different standards of scrutiny. Schlozman and Tierney, *Organized Interests*, 295–97.

16. Jeffrey M. Berry, *Lobbying for the People: The Political Behavior of Public Interest Groups* (Princeton, N.J.: Princeton University Press, 1977), 223.

17. Sherral Brown-Guinyard and Ashlyn K. Kuersten, "Coalition Building: Race- and Gender-Based Groups as Amicus Curiae in the United States Supreme Court" (paper presented at the annual meeting of the American Political Science Association, New York, 2 September 1994), 12.

18. For an anecdotal but insightful examination of this question, see Burdett A. Loomis, "Coalitions of Interests: Building Bridges in the Balkanized State," in *Interest Group Politics*, 2d ed., ed. Allan J. Cigler and Burdett A. Loomis (Washington, D.C.: Congressional Quarterly Press, 1986), 264–66.

19. See, specifically, Douglas W. Costain and Anne N. Costain, "Interest Groups as Policy Aggregators in the Legislative Process," *Polity* 14, no. 2 (winter 1981): 249–72. For other, briefer discussions, see Kay Lehman Schlozman and John T. Tierney, *Organized Interests*, 307; Christopher Bosso, *Pesticides and Politics: The Life Cycle of a Public Issue* (Pittsburgh: University of Pittsburgh Press, 1987), 233; Hugh Heclo, "The Changing Presidential Office," in *The Managerial Presidency*, ed. James P. Pfiffner (Pacific Grove, Calif.: Brooks/Cole Publishing Co., 1991), 40.

20. And, as I also argued in chapter 4, specialists who find themselves unable to piggyback their issues onto coalition structures are likely to leave the coalition altogether.

CHAPTER 8

1. Marie Hojnacki, "Interest Groups' Decisions to Join Alliances or Work Alone," *American Journal of Political Science* 41, no. 1 (January 1997):82.

2. Kay Lehman Schlozman and John T. Tierney, *Organized Interests and American Democracy* (New York: Harper and Row, 1986), 283–88; Robert H. Salisbury, John P. Heinz, Edward O. Laumann, and Robert L. Nelson, "Who Works with Whom? Interest Group Alliances and Opposition," *American Political Science Review* 81 (1987): 1217–34.

3. Jeffrey M. Berry, "Subgovernments, Issue Networks, and Political Conflict," in *Remaking American Politics*, ed. Richard A. Harris and Sidney M. Milkis (Boulder, Colo.: Westview Press, 1989), 239–60.

4. On the general issue of belief congruence between interest group elites and membership, see Paul A. Sabatier and Susan M. McLaughlin, "Belief Congruence of Governmental and Interest Group Elites with Their Constituencies," *American Politics Quarterly* 16, no. 1 (January 1988): 61–98; Paul A. Sabatier and Susan M. McLaughlin, "Belief Congruence between Interest-Group Leaders and Members: An Empirical Analysis of Three Theories and a Suggested Synthesis," *Journal of Politics* 52, no. 3 (August 1990): 914–35.

5. Hojnacki, "Interest Groups' Decisions," 81–82.

6. Ibid. 84.

7. William P. Browne, "Organized Interests and Their Issue Niches: A Search for Pluralism in a Policy Domain," *Journal of Politics* 52 (May 1990): 477–509; William P. Browne, "Issue Niches and the Limits of Interest Group Influence," in *Interest Group Politics*, 3d ed., ed. Allan J. Cigler and Burdett A. Loomis (Washington, D.C.: Congressional Quarterly Press, 1991), 345–70. See also Hojnacki's comments on Browne's work in "Interest Groups' Decisions," 84 n.

8. William P. Browne, "Issue Niches and the Limits of Interest Group Influence," 353.

9. David Knoke, *Organizing for Collective Action: The Political Economies of Associations* (New York: Aldine de Gruyter, 1990), 210–12.

10. The survey item read: "Here is a list of issues. Could you tell me which of these policy areas your organization is *particularly* active in?" The policy domains included agriculture, civil rights, consumer rights, defense, domestic economic policy, education, energy, environmental policy, foreign policy, health, housing, international trade, labor policy, law enforcement, social welfare/social security, transportation, urban development, other.

11. Charles Lindblom, *Politics and Markets* (New York: Basic Books, 1977), 175.

12. For the role of achieving a "critical mass" in collective action, see Pamela Oliver, Gerald Marwell, and Ruy Teixeira, "A Theory of the Critical Mass. I. Interdependence Group Heterogeneity, and the Production of Collective Action," *American Journal of Sociology* 91, no. 3 (November 1985): 522–56; Pamela E. Oliver and Gerald Marwell, "The Paradox of Group Size in Collective Action: A Theory of the Critical Mass. II," *American Sociological Review* 53 (February 1988): 1–8; Gerald Marwell, Pamela E. Oliver, and Ralph Prahl,

"Social Networks and Collective Action: A Theory of the Critical Mass. III," *American Journal of Sociology* 94, no. 3 (November 1988): 501–34.

CHAPTER 9

1. On the connection between collective action, electronic communication, and transaction costs, see Mark S. Bonchek, "Grassroots in Cyberspace: Recruiting Members on the Internet" (paper presented at the 53rd Annual Meeting of the Midwest Political Science Association, Chicago, 6–8 April 1995).

2. Charles Lindblom, *Politics and Markets* (New York: Basic Books, 1977), 175.

3. Constance Ewing Cook, *Lobbying for Higher Education: How Colleges and Universities Influence Federal Policy* (Nashville: Vanderbilt University Press, 1998), 162.

4. James Madison, "The Federalist No. 10," in *The Federalist*, ed. Jacob E. Cooke (Middletown, Conn.: Wesleyan University Press, 1961), 57.

5. Madison, "The Federalist No. 51," in *The Federalist*, 351.

6. With all due respect to Schattschneider's comment that the "flaw in the pluralist heaven is that the heavenly chorus sings with a strong upper-class accent." E. E. Schattschneider, *The Semisovereign People: A Realist's View of Democracy in America* (1960; reprint, Hinsdale, Ill.: Dryden Press, 1975), 34–35.

7. David R. Mayhew, *Congress: The Electoral Connection* (New Haven: Yale University Press, 1974); Richard F. Fenno, Jr., *Home Style: House Members in Their Districts* (Boston: Little, Brown, 1978).

8. Hugh Heclo, "Issue Networks and the Executive Establishment," in *The New American Political System*, ed. Anthony King (Washington, D.C.: American Enterprise Institute, 1978), 97.

Index

ACTION (ACTIvism ONline), 89
activities: defined, 97; importance of, and
    coalition strategies, 103–107; policy,
    95–101; political, 95–101; political, and
    policy compared, 97–100, 127;
    symbolic, 36–37, 48
adversaries, 6, 53–54, 92
agendas, formation of, 52; shaping,
    30–32, 44–46, 124
airlines, 2, 5–6, 13, 14
Air Transport Association, 109
Aircraft Owners and Pilots Association,
    53, 109
allies, 6; characteristics of, 45;
    identification of potential, 51–55, 61, 63
American Airlines, 14
American Arts Alliance, 89
American Association of State Highway
    and Transportation Officials, 14
American Bus Association, 14
American Civil Liberties Union, 89
American Council on Education, 67
American Trucking Association, 59
American Vocational Association, 67
Americans with Disabilities Act, 160n.
    38, 165n. 6 (ch. 5)
amicus curiae briefs, 99
Arco, 89
associations, proliferation of, 3
atomization, 3, 5, 26, 59, 128; and
    interlocks, 69
attorneys, outside, 69–72

Bauer, Raymond A., 28
BellSouth, 89
benefits: information, 7, 23, 34–35, 46, 66,
    94, 123; professional, 25, 38; purposive,
    161n. 4; reputation as, 95; selective,
    22–23, 38, 46, 122–23; symbolic, 7, 23,

35–37, 48, 94, 123, 124, 125. *See also*
    incentives
Berry, Jeffrey M., 26, 27, 98–99
Big Six, 15, 132; identified, 159n. 21
Boeing, 2, 134
brokers, of coalitions, 8, 38, 109, 157n. 24;
    as core groups, 41–42; and information
    challenges, 51, 54; and peripheral
    groups, 47; and reputation incentives,
    106; and technology, 89, 91
Brown-Guinyard, Sherral, 99
Browne, William P., 10, 26, 95, 111, 112
businesses, links between, 74, 128–129;
    privileged position of, 118, 127;
    representation in Washington, 2–3, 27,
    74; resources of, 127, 129
Bykerk, Loree, 10

Campaign to Stop the U.S.
    Communications Decency Act, 89
campaigns, group participation in, 96,
    127
Capitol Advantage, 89
Career College Association, 89
career path. *See* revolving door
case studies, 10
Central Intelligence Agency, 169n. 20
cheap riding, 25
China, 2, 134
Cigler, Allan J., 12
civil rights, characteristics of domain,
    15–16; and coalition behavior
    summarized, 130–31
Clark, Peter B., 23
Clinton, Bill, 1, 88
Coalition for Networked Information, 88
Coalition for Vehicle Choice, 89
coalitions: defined, 22, 155n. 4; financing,
    48; as frequent strategy, 3; long-term, 5;

175